Mens Sana
in Thingummy Doodah

Victoria Wood is the writer and star of the two *As Seen On TV* series, followed by a *TV Special* and *An Audience With Victoria Wood* which won BAFTA awards for Best Light Entertainment Programme in 1985, 1986, 1987 and 1988. She has performed a series of one woman shows in theatres all over Britain, including the London Palladium in 1987 and the Strand Palace Theatre in 1990. Her previous books, *Lucky Bag: The Victoria Wood Song Book*; *Up To You, Porky: The Victoria Wood Sketch Book* and *Barmy: The New Victoria Wood Sketch Book* were based on her stage and television shows.

In 1989 she created a new series of six TV shows which are featured in this collection, *Mens Sana in Thingummy Doodah*. She is one of Britain's wittiest, most popular and best loved comedians and comic writers.

'Unlike other comedy scripts, which rely on slight gags and actor interpretation to make the writing come alive, Victoria Wood's work is almost as funny on the page as on the screen'

City Limits

Victoria Wood

MENS SANA IN THINGUMMY DOODAH
and Five Other
Nuggets of
Homely Fun

Mandarin

by the same author
Lucky Bag: The Victoria Wood Song Book
Up To You, Porky: The Victoria Wood Sketch Book
Barmy: The New Victoria Wood Sketch Book

MENS SANA IN THINGUMMY DOODAH
First ublished in Great Britain in 1991 by Methuen London

First published in paperback in 1991 by Mandarin Paperbacks
Michelin House, 81 Fulham Road, London SW3 6RB

Mandarin is an imprint of the Octopus Group

ISBN 07493 0818 4
A CIP catalogue record for this book
is available from the British Library

Photographs for 'Mens Sana in Thingummy Doodah',
'The Library', 'We Would Quite
Like to Apologise', 'Over to Pam'
and 'Staying in' by Don Smith.
Photographs for 'Val de Ree' by Chris Ridley.
All reproduced courtesy of the *Radio Times*.

Printed and bound in Great Britain by
BPCC Hazell Books
Aylesbury, Bucks, England
Member of BPCC Ltd.

To all the Old Bags in Equity,
most of whom were in
this series

Contents

List of Illustrations

Preface: How a television series is made   1

Mens Sana in Thingummy Doodah   5

The Library   33

We Would Quite Like to Apologise   61

Over to Pam   87

Val de Ree   111

Staying in   137

Cast List   163

List of Illustrations

Page

6	Victoria Wood
9	Julie Walters
14	Victoria Wood and Lill Roughley
20	Victoria Wood, Lill Roughley, Meg Johnson and Anne Reid
22	Victoria Wood and Lill Roughley
34	Victoria Wood and Anne Reid
38	Victoria Wood and Anne Reid
40	Victoria Wood and Anne Reid
42	Victoria Wood and Anne Reid
44	Victoria Wood, Anne Reid and Philip Lowrie
58	Victoria Wood and Danny O'Dea
62	Victoria Wood
72	Lill Roughley, Julie Walters, Victoria Wood, Una Stubbs
88	Victoria Wood and Julie Walters
104	Victoria Wood
112	Celia Imrie and Victoria Wood
116	Victoria Wood and Celia Imrie
127	Victoria Wood and Celia Imrie
131	Joan Sims
138	Victoria Wood
144	Victoria Wood, Patricia Hodge and Jim Broadbent
147	Celia Imrie, Victoria Wood and Susie Blake
150	John Nettleton, Victoria Wood, Roger Brierley and Phyllis Calvert
153	Richard Lintern, Patricia Hodge, Victoria Wood and Brian Burdon
160	Victoria Wood and Patricia Hodge
160	Victoria Wood and Patricia Hodge
160	Victoria Wood and Patricia Hodge

How a television series is made

Hello! I thought I would tell you all about how a television series is made. It's very exciting! It all begins a long time ago when the Writer – she is an irritable person with bitten nails – gets a Red Telephone Bill. This sets the Writer thinking, and not so very long later she has written a television series! This is a collection of six 'programmes', either with a gap in the middle for a cup of tea, or a guaranteed repeat, depending on whether it is a commercial 'programme' or a BBC one. This particular television series is a BBC one, so we will have to wait till it is over for our cup of tea, won't we?

Once the Writer has finished writing, she takes the 'script' and drives through a traffic jam in the rain to the Typist. The Typist is a grim woman in a balaclava who makes jokes like, 'Well it doesn't make me laugh,' and, 'Don't mind the dog, it should come off with a nailbrush.'

When 'scripts' are typed, the Writer takes them to the BBC where a seventeen-year-old Secretary spills coffee on them and leaves them behind the photocopier. When the Secretary leaves the BBC to become a full-time sunbather it can sometimes be a jolly long time before those 'scripts' come to light! And sometimes when they do they have been hidden for such a long time they have become 'dated' and 'unrealistic'. But fortunately, the BBC will still make them into 'programmes'.

Then the fun begins! All is hustle and bustle in the office as the 'production team' begins to assemble. Oh look – there is the Production Secretary. My goodness, she's busy! She knows everything about the show that is about to be made. Surrounded by wallplans and telephones, she is a real hub of activity. She has three fags going in the ashtray, and a fourth is singeing her bi-focals, but we'd better not tell her, had we? We would get our heads bitten off!

Here come the Producer and the Director. They are both men, and my goodness they drink a lot of tea! Thank heavens they have a Production Secretary or they'd have to make it themselves! And that would never do!

Hello, here's the Designer. He is bringing in a 'model' of the 'set'. The Writer has written a programme 'set' in a Welsh kitchen. The 'model' is of a shopping centre and multi-storey carpark. Oh well, never mind!

Well, now everyone has had plenty of tea and hidden the cups all round the office. The Production Secretary will have fun trying to find them all! Shall we help her? No. We would get our heads bitten off!

Now the fun really begins! We have to find some 'Actors and Actresses' to appear in our 'programmes'. The Production Secretary could do this perfectly well, but she's busy washing up so let's phone up the 'Casting Director'. She is a lady in funny shoes who can remember some of the names of half of the people she's seen in the theatre. While she's trying to remember the others, let's have another cup of tea! Oh honestly, where on earth is that Production Secretary? She'd better turn up soon, or the Producer will be cross!

Well, now we have some Actors and Actresses. The ones we really wanted were all busy or asked for lots of money, but I expect these ones will do jolly well, don't you?

Now the fun is really hotting up! Everybody meets up in a condemned council block called the BBC Rehearsal Rooms. This morning we are having a 'read through', but first we have to get past the Security Man. And, oh dear, he's not in a very good mood this morning. He hasn't heard of any of our Actors and Actresses! Never mind, let's leave the Production Secretary to sort it out while we have a nice cup of tea!

Now fun is really on the agenda! Everybody sits round a big table. They are all very nervous but the Producer goes to the lavatory and soon everyone is chatting away like billy-oh! It's time to read out the whole script from top to bottom. It is a long time since the Writer first had that Red Telephone Bill and she is dying to hear how the 'dialogue' will sound when acted by real Actors and Actresses. When they have finished everyone is very pleased. Didn't they think of some nice funny voices? Everybody has been so clever, the Writer has had to go to the window and think what a long way it would be to jump down onto the main road. Ouch! That would hurt, wouldn't it?

Now 'rehearsals' are all over, and it's nearly time for
the 'recording'. What fun that will be! Now we will find
out exactly how funny our 'programme' is! Look – here
comes the audience! Hurry up, slowcoaches! Goodness
me, what a lot of walking frames! Somebody is grumbling
that his hearing aid is faulty and he didn't want to come out
anyway. Never mind, the Actors will just have to speak up,
won't they?

Now the 'warm-up' starts. And oh, it is fun! What nice
slacks the Warm-up Man is wearing! The audience do enjoy
his jokes. You can see them nudging each other. 'What is a
pouf?' they ask.

Now the 'recording' is underway and the audience is having
a lovely time. They are looking at the cameras, the lights, the
doorway, in fact everywhere except at the poor Actors and
Actresses. Never mind; let's all shout louder and see if we can
make them laugh that way.

Once the 'programme' is 'in the can' the fun really begins!
Our audience were having such a good time they forgot to
laugh! Never mind, let's switch on this clever machine that
sounds almost like an audience laughing. Let's turn it up
really loud, then everyone will know just how funny our
'programme' is. The Writer is pleased. Now no one can hear
the Actors and Actresses getting their 'dialogue' wrong.
That's a relief!

Now the 'programme' is on the 'television'. I hope
everybody likes it. Thank heavens there are three other
channels! James Bond is on one of them. I wonder which
channel people will watch tonight?

Now 'television' has closed down for the night, and all the
people who write for the newspapers are settling down to tell
everybody just what they think of our 'programme'. Now the
fun really begins!

Mens Sana
in Thingummy Doodah

Mens Sana in Thingummy Doodah

Old country house in its grounds, very imposing but maybe a little run down. Signboard says Pinkney Hydro – Your Gateway to to Health. *Lill and Victoria are getting their bags out of the car, locking it, and going up the steps to the front entrance. Lill is a bit overweight; a bit run down and frazzled-looking.*

Entrance hall of the Hydro: modern reception desk amidst chipped statuary and grubbily carpeted staircase. Lill and Victoria stand with their bags, looking around.

Lill	It looked nice in the brochure.
Victoria	Chernobyl looked nice in the brochure.
Lill	Well – somewhere through there is a team of dedicated professionals, lean, fit, health conscious, ready to help me achieve my full potential in mind and body.

Dana, huge, nineteen, in filthy overall, thunders down the staircase holding a washing-up bowl full of wet greens and a sink plunger. She is shouting up to someone on the upper landing (unseen).

Dana	If the lard comes, put it next to the pig-bin. *(Stops. Looks up.)* Eh? *(Pause)* Well just blow the hairs off it. Sorry – I didn't see you. Is it Miss Wood and Miss Sutcliffe?
Victoria	Yes
Dana	D'you want to come up? Everyone's out ont' Health and Nature Trail.
Lill	Oh that sounds nice, doesn't it?
Dana	It's just a load of hopping over logs really.

She goes upstairs, they follow her.

	Anyway, I'm Dana.
Lill	Unusual name.
Dana	My mother's favourite singer when she fell pregnant. I were lucky. My brother's called Harry Secombe. Anyway, I'm head cook and carrot scrubber – so – *(stops outside door and opens it)* this is it. Your bathroom's *en suite* with it all; there's no emergency bell but we can be summoned by a thump. Er, your flush is dicky, but it responds to patience and don't run the bidet and that cold tap simultaneous or you'll scorch your nancy. Any chocolates, booze, fags?
Both	No.
Dana	Right. Calorie-wise, you're now under orders till checkout.
Lill	Right. Good.
Dana	And we'll see you downstairs in half an hour for an introductory blah-blah – yeah?
Victoria	OK.
Dana	*(leaving, singing)* Oooh-eee, chirpy chirpy cheep cheep. . .

They go into the room. It is a twin-bedded, smallish, nastyish hotel room; modern fittings with old windows and curtains etc. Victoria is on the bed looking out of the window; Lill is unpacking.

Victoria	What's it for?
Lill	What?
Victoria	Candlewick.
Lill	What do you mean?
Victoria	Well it doesn't look nice, or feel nice – it must have *some* other purpose. I think it was probably invented in the war –
Lill	Like Spam?
Victoria	No. Like Morse Code. As a method of passing cryptic messages – it's all in the pattern – two tufts and a wiggly bit mean 'Watch Out – Vera Lynn is touring North Africa'.
Lill	I shouldn't have said Spam.
Victoria	Why?
Lill	Well I want some, now I know I can't have any.

Victoria	Well go and get some.
Lill	This is a health farm! I'm here to detoxify, lose weight. It's not going to work very well if I'm nipping out every two minutes for a quarter of potted meat.
Victoria	Sorry.
Lill	This week is crucial to my whole future way of life, and I will need your full and unstinting support and encouragement to make this vital project a success.
Victoria	Right.
Lill	Do you understand?
Victoria	Yep.
Lill	Do you have anything to say?
Victoria	Yep.
Lill	What?
Victoria	Spam Spam Spam Spam Spam! Chips! Nougat! Chocolate!

The main reception room has also seen better days. Oil paintings, ping-pong table, sofas, coffee tables abound. A group of residents, including Victoria, Lill, Connie, Enid, and various rheumatic and overweight older people, are listening to Nicola who is slim, thirty-five-ish, very sincere and softly-spoken.

Nicola	OK, everybody, I'm Nicola. I'm just calling you 'everybody' because I don't know everybody's name as yet, and until me doing that, 'everybody' as a sort of termitude will have to huffice. I'm Nicola, as I say; if you should need me at all during the periodical which you're with us, just examine a member of staff who's approximate, say 'Where's Nicola' and that will find me. This is the Pinkney Hydro, as you'll have gathered, the gateway *to* health. I don't know if you're familiar with the old Latin saying – I only speak a little Latin myself, just enough to buy a paper – the saying 'Mens Sana Incorporises' And I think we can learn a lot from that. I've only recently taken over as head of Pinkneys, but don't despair, I do have a full and variable business career behind of me, including hands-on salon experience galore plus two years of prosthetic nail work. I'm Nicola, as I say, and this here standing alongside of

myself is Judy. Judy is more to deal with the physical aspects of the body; aerobics, jogging and our very own Pinkneys specialité de la hydro, Ping-pong Mobility. Judy will be explaining of that as and when and so forth. . . . As well as Judy and myself we do have a highly professional team of, of professionals, who will be intending to your needs should they arise. *(Looks down at notes.)*

Victoria   *(mouthing to Lill)* Where are they?

Nicola   Our aim here at Pinkneys is very simple, erm, it's to do with intoxifying the body, treating the body as a temple, I hope that doesn't offend anybody, I say 'temple' but I could just have easily as said 'garden centre' – they're very popular of a Sunday, aren't they; and losing weight and perhaps trying a face pack or something – anyway – I'm Nicola. Thank you. As I say.

The dining room: tables for four and five scattered about. A few people are already sitting waiting, including Victoria and Lill at a table for four. Lill is in a dressing gown, Victoria in a track suit.

Lill   Well, my massage was marvellous. I feel really relaxed. And my masseur, Harold –

Victoria   You can't have a masseur called Harold. It's like having a member of the Royal Family called Ena.

Lill   Harold says that underneath my fat, I'm actually very slim.

Victoria   He sounds very intelligent.

Lill   And an extra daily massage with him –

Victoria   At twenty pounds.

Lill   At twenty pounds – should really make a difference.

Victoria   Well my girl was hopeless. She's only here because she didn't get enough CSEs to work in a pet shop. Every time she said S she spat on my hair.

Lill   That doesn't matter.

Victoria   It does if she's telling you about Somerset. I had to change the subject to Peterborough.

Connie and Enid come over to the table; fiftyish, glamorous, in track suits and high-heeled mules.

Connie	Can we park? Are you bothered?
Victoria	Help yourselves.
Connie	Connie and Enid. We're old Pinkney partners from way back.
Victoria	You've been here before?
Connie	Bushels of occasions, haven't we?
Enid	Oh, at least.
Connie	First time since it changed hands, but last year it really was fandabbidozy and how.
Lill	Do you come to lose weight?
Enid	And tone.
Connie	Trim and tone. Enid has underarm swoop and I have runaway midriff.
Lill	You look very good to me, actually; both of you.
Enid	Well, I like to keep at it. I was Slimmer of the Month in February.
Connie	The February we went decimal.
Enid	It isn't food with me, like it is with Connie, I have water retention.
Connie	You've perhaps heard Hereford's missing a reservoir?
Enid	Connie's having acupuncture. For stress-related gobbling.
Connie	Enid's not been offered it, naturally. Well, acupuncture and water retention – you'd be forever swabbing the lino. How about you?
Lill	Well – today is the first day of the rest of my life.
Connie	Oh! It's the first day of Lewis's sale. Beggar. Go on.
Lill	I want a complete new start – hair, face, body, psyche . . .
Enid	Are you?
Lill	Sorry?
Enid	Are you psychic?
Lill	No I'm not.
Enid	Oh. Only my mother's haunting our spare-room blanket box and I could do with having it exorcised.
Connie	Trust your mother. Whole of Paradise to choose from, she plumps for your blanket box. She was the same in Fuengirola. Five-bedroom luxury villa, girls. Spent the whole holiday rinsing dishcloths.

Dana comes in with four small glass bowls of brown slop.

Victoria	Thanks.
Dana	Don't leave it all at once.
Victoria	What is it?
Dana	Bran, another sort of bran, wheatgerm, apple juice and sultana.
Enid	Sultanas?
Dana	Sultana.
Victoria	Is it good for you?
Dana	Haven't a clue, but don't spill it – it sets. *(She leaves, singing.)* All kinds of everything, remind me of you . . .

They eat, gingerly.

Their bedroom. Lill is staring at her face in the dressing-table mirror. Victoria is on the bed with a chart.

Victoria	Lill!
Lill	I'm sorry; it's the wheatgerm. What have we got this afternoon?
Victoria	I'm having twenty minutes in the thermal cabinet and you're having your legs waxed, then we're meeting up for passive exercise.
Lill	I'm going to be a new woman when I leave here – this is going to be the turnround in my relationship with Marcus.
Victoria	Why?
Lill	Well, I think when he sees me all well-groomed and slim, and confident, I really think he might re-consider divorcing Petra.
Victoria	But why do you want him to?
Lill	I've been in love with Marcus for twelve years, you know.
Victoria	But he's awful, Lill. His wife is called Petra; he chose to spend his life with a woman who has the same name as John Noakes's labrador.
Lill	He loves me. He's just waiting till the children are settled.

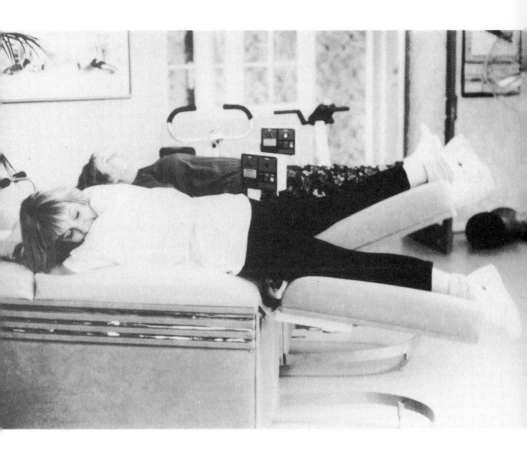

Victoria	What in – sheltered housing? God, I'm starving – how many calories in a pillowcase?
Lill	Plain or Oxford.
Victoria	What's for dinner?
Lill	*(consulting the plan)* Clear vegetable soup and cruditics.
Victoria	Bum, willy, toilet –

Lill looks at her.

Sorry, I'm so hungry I'm having mine now.

The Gym. Lill and Victoria are both on passive exercisers – electronically controlled couches that do all the exercise for you. Lill's is doing sit ups and Victoria's is working her legs. Sallyanne, a model, is sitting on a rowing machine examining her split ends.

Lill	So what's the diet?
Sallyanne	Well, what it is you do – you eat a hard-boiled egg before every meal, and the hard-boiled egg actually eats some of that meal for you. And so you lose weight.

They all think about this.

Victoria	You don't want to lose weight, do you?
Sallyanne	I do, Victoria. My agent says if I can't taper my hips to quite an extent I can say bye-bye lingerie, hello bakeware.
Victoria	Are you a model?
Sallyanne	Catalogues, glamour and promos. Have you seen the Car Parts Calendar?
Victoria	Er –
Sallyanne	I'm August. I'm pointing at a fanbelt.
Victoria	Was that topless?
Sallyanne	Not really, I was holding quite a big spanner.
Lill	Course, they say you shouldn't eat a lot of eggs now, don't they?
Sallyanne	Quite honestly, Lill, if you believed everything they tell you – like all this 'other people smoking can give you cancer' – I mean how can it – if you read

	a book, Victoria, that's not going to make me more intelligent, is it?
Victoria	I wouldn't have thought so.
Sallyanne	No. And look at the moaning over the Greenhouse Effect – the terrible weather we have in this country, you'd think people would be pleased – I'm buying a barbecue. People knock Mrs Thatcher but, good heavens, Victoria, three hours' sleep a night and her suits are immaculate, and that new hairstyle gives her whole face a lift – I think we could do with something like the Falklands again actually, don't you – something British – give us all a rally round . . . *(She gets up.)*
Victoria	See you later.
Sallyanne	In a while, alligator. *(Leaves.)*
Victoria	I can't believe we're doing this, Lill. I can't believe we've paid three hundred and fifty pounds to drink hot water and be strapped to an out-of-control sofa.
Lill	Well if it gives me a waist like Sallyanne, it's absolutely worth it.
Victoria	If it gives you a brain like Sallyanne you'll have room for a handbag under your skull.
Lill	*(getting off her machine)* Right, that's me finished. You're on this one now.
Victoria	Am I? *(Gets on it.)* What does this one do for me?
Lill	It narrows the waist and flattens the abdomen.
Victoria	Oh yeah?
Lill	If you stay on it long enough.
Victoria	Could be a long time. I can see all the chaps at the Central Electicity Generating Board with their coats on, going 'Oh blimey – is she still on it?'

Judy marches in, clipboard at the ready.

Judy	Early morning jog: takers?
Lill	Now, what does jogging do for you exactly?
Judy	*(miming)* Circulation, stamina, hah hah hah hah and muscle. *(She slaps her stomach.)*
Lill	Really? Which muscles is it good for then?
Judy	Tip top for hams, gluts, pecs, abs –
Victoria	And you speak Esperanto!
Lill	Sorry, I didn't catch all the names –

Judy	Well, pop into my eyrie if you'd like more gen.
Lill	OK.
Judy	I've a selection of full-colour diagrams of the major muscle groups – thrilling!
Lill	Right. So you think jogging's definitely a good thing?
Judy	Not a doubt in my mind. I jog – I'm strong, I'm fit. I haven't blown my nose since 1973 and I have an extremely regular and satisfactory bowel movement.
Victoria	Got any diagrams of that?
Judy	So – yes to jogging?
Lill	Yes, I think I should.
Judy	I agrcc. *(Pokes Lill's leg.)* Tighten these wobblers.

Victoria laughs.

Lill	Put us both down.

Judy moves to the door.

Victoria	What?
Judy	*(stopping in doorway)* Six forty-five – patio – warm up – yes?
Victoria	What are you trying to do to me? Six forty-five is a time for dreaming that Woody Allen has popped round with a picnic hamper: it is not a time for assembling on a patio with a load of eager beavers in mesh sleeveless blouses.
Lill	It'll release all your tensions.
Victoria	It will not. I shall be all knotted up wondering how I can kick you up the bum without breaking my stride.
Lill	*(switching Vic's machine on)* I shall see you at Happy Hour.

She leaves.

Victoria	Happy Hour? Huh! Two cups of Marmite for the price of one.

A pause while the machine works. Two maintenance men come in; a big middle-aged one and a lad. They stare at Victoria's machine intently, bending

*down to look at the mechanism. They take no
notice of her.*

Older Man Thought so . . .

He straightens up and looks at watch.

Come on, Allardyce; brew time.

They leave. Victoria is left on the machine.

Victoria I see that was Allardyce.

*The dining room. Victoria, Lill, Sallyanne, Connie and
Enid are finishing their meal. They're at the herb tea
stage. Dana comes to their table with a Thermos jug.*

Dana More hot water, slaves?
Victoria Can I have another tea bag?
Dana Can you bog roll. Nothing more now till brekkers.
Enid You can top me up, Dana.
Lill Oh, we're on early breakfast.
Victoria Oh yes, miss, early breakfast for us, miss, we're going
jogging.
Connie Catch me.
Enid You've come adrift, Dana, cleavage-wise.
Dana *(buttoning herself up)* Blinking Allardyce. I said to him,
I don't mind what you do with them but put them back
after. Tuh. *(She goes off singing:)* Gimme gimme gimme
dat, gimme dat ding . . . *(She turns at the doorway.)* I
mean, I'd do the same with his flies, wouldn't I? *(Sings:)*
Gimme dat ding . . .
Victoria And she chops our coleslaw!
Connie Talk about Now Wash Your Hands.
Sallyanne I've seen that somewhere. Is it a film?

Nicola comes in.

Nicola Oh hello – everybody. I hope you all enjoyed your
crudities. Nicola here. I'm afraid we don't have an
organised activity as such on the agendum. We were

	hoping to have a twilight display of mouth-to-mouth resuscitation in the treatment lobby.
Connie	*(knowingly)* Resus.
Nicola	But Mrs Fernihough can't be here, she had a slight accident and scratched her Volvo. But activities will have resumed by tomorrow and we'll be circling a pamphlet to that intention so you can exercise your choosing as and whenever. I hope you haven't found the first day's regiment too astringent – I know camomile isn't everyone's cup of tea – but do stick with it and results will turn themselves up shortly. So. Bye.

She goes out.

Connie	Nice enough woman, but nothing on sale in the brain department.
Enid	Not even a special purchase.
Sallyanne	I'm going to wash my hair again. I've got a shampoo with herbs in that mends split ends.
Victoria	How can it?
Sallyanne	How can it?
Victoria	How can it mend them?
Sallyanne	How can it mend what? Sorry?
Victoria	How can it mend split ends?
Sallyanne	My shampoo?
Victoria	Yes. How can it mend them?
Sallyanne	It's got herbs in.
Victoria	What do they do?
Sallyanne	They mend the split ends. See you later.

Sallyanne leaves.

Victoria	What's on telly tonight?
Connie	There's no telly at Pinkneys.
Enid	You're supposed to be getting away from it all. The hurly-burly of modern living.
Victoria	But I like hurly-burly. Especially burly.
Lill	Well, I'm going on the rowing machine, I think.
Connie	Come on, Enid; face-pack time.
Lill	*(eagerly)* Are they good?
Connie	It shuts her up yapping, so it suits me.

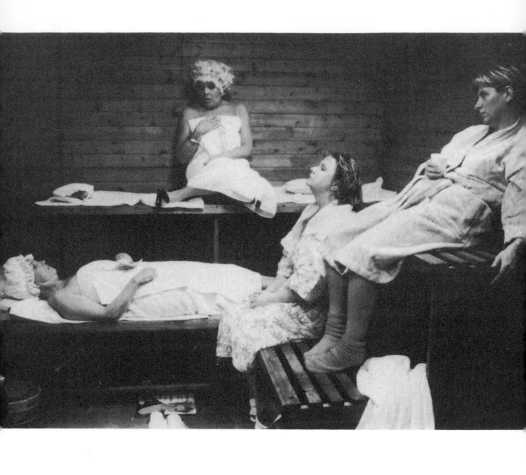

Connie, Enid and Lill prepare to go.

Victoria   Are there any books?

Connie   There's a *Readers Digest* in the treatment lobby. What was that piece, Enid?

Enid   'How I scaled Kilimanjaro without a Spleen'. Night night.

The three of them leave. Victoria spots a forgotten cauliflower floret and eats it.

Victoria   I'm fed up.

The patio, early next morning. Victoria, Lill, a couple of silent men and one very fit-looking elderly lady are bending and stretching to Judy's orders.

Judy   OK. Follow me. Brisk walk to begin.

Victoria   I hate you, Lillian Sutcliffe. I hate everybody here. I hate the sky. I hate my eyelids.

Lill   It'll get you fit.

Victoria   What am I getting fit for? I'm never going to do this again. Jogging is for people who aren't intelligent enough to watch breakfast television.

Judy   And *jog*!

Lill   Suppose you have to run for a bus?

Victoria   I'll wait for the next one.

Lill   It lifts your buttocks.

Victoria   I don't want them lifted; I'm quite happy with them bobbling along where they are.

Lill   Well I know Marcus would prefer mine a little higher.

Victoria   Well have plastic surgery. They could probably convert them into shoulder pads.

(Both are getting out of breath.)

And anyway, Marcus is hardly Michelangelo's David. And as for that thing he wears on his head . . .

Lill   It's a very expensive hairpiece.

Victoria	He should ask for a refund. I've seen more convincing toupés grown on a wet flannel.

Judy and the others forge ahead.

Judy	Come on, slackers – put your backs in.

They stagger on. Victoria looks at Lill.

Victoria	Oh, Lill, you haven't! Not again!
Lill	It must be the raw broccoli.
Victoria	I wouldn't mind, I can't even open a window.

The dining room a little later. Dana is laying tables.
Victoria and Lill stagger up to their table, breathless.

Victoria	Where's breakfast?
Dana	There.
Lill	Where?
Dana	On t' table.
Victoria	There's only hot water here.
Dana	That's it.
Victoria	That's breakfast?
Dana	You're fasting today; did Nicola not say?
Victoria	No.
Dana	Ne'er mind. Tomorrow's Grape Nuts. *(She sings:)* Every sha la la la la, Every who oh oh oh . . .
Lill	Well – when I stand in the registry office with Marcus by my side this will all be worth it.
Victoria	While you're there – could you register my death?

The sauna. Connie, Enid and Victoria are laid out on
shelves. Lill comes in and arranges herself.

Lill	You know, I think Sallyanne's shampoo really works – I don't seem to have half so many split ends today.
Victoria	Oh please, Lill. You'll be holding your sheets up to the window next.
Enid	*(reading from a magazine)* What's wrong with this? Problem page: I am at the end of my tether – my husband is important.

Connie	Impotent!
Enid	What's that when it's gone shopping?
Connie	No oomph. Bed-wise.
Enid	Eh?
Connie	The escalator doesn't reach the underpant department.
Enid	Not with it.
Connie	Explain, Victoria.
Victoria	Well, you know celery –
Enid	Do I know celery? Widnes Central Slimmer of the Month – I could make an edge-to-edge jerkin out of celery and still have enough to stiffen a roller blind. What do you mean, though, re celery?
Lill	It's a sexual problem, Enid.
Enid	*(losing interest)* Oh. I thought it was something interesting.
Lill	Marcus can't always . . . you know.
Victoria	Well you can't concentrate when you're wearing a toupé. It's like trying to play *Monopoly* with a paper hat on.
Connie	Is this your chap, Lill? Marcus?
Lill	I'm hoping he'll divorce his wife.
Connie	Mm, I kept hoping mine would – and I *was* his wife. He passed away in Cleveleys, so that saved a solicitor.
Lill	Don't you miss him?
Connie	I prefer my independence.
Victoria	See!
Connie	I've never done anything with a man that was more fun than rummy.

Lill sighs.

Victoria	What's on tonight, Enid?
Enid	*(looking at pamphlet)* A talk – 'Corsetry Thro' the Ages'. Nicola gave me a taster over breakfast. Apparently Mary Queen of Scots –
Connie	What – *the* Mary Queen of Scots?
Enid	Mm – her in the necklace. She apparently was wearing something very like our modern brassière the day she was beheaded.

Connie	That's pitiful, isn't it. If it had been halter-neck the chopper might have bounced off the elastic.
Enid	I love historical people, don't you? Cleopatra, Florence Nightingale, Noële Gordon –
Victoria	She wasn't historical. She was an actress.
Enid	I don't mean Noële Gordon. I mean Edith Cavell.
Victoria	What's on tomorrow night?
Enid	Barndancing with Kirsty.
Connie	They can stuff that, for me: barndancing. They can stuff it in a pastry case and glaze it. For me.
Enid	And me. That Kirsty's never set foot in a barn. Obviously been no nearer a barn than a gingham wrap around. Kirsty's much more of a hip hop and scratch merchant.
Connie	You'll be hip hop and scratch if you don't shift it – herbal rubs at half past.

Connie and Enid prepare to leave.

Victoria	What's that?
Connie	Gordon only knows. I just hope it's not parsley.
Enid	Ooh so do I. Parsley's my pet noir.

They start to leave, mumbling.

Enid	Where's my bandanna, Connie?
Connie	How the figgy pudding should I know – I'm not a bandanna warden . . .

Judy bursts in.

Judy	Come on, come on! Aerobics! Gymnasium two minutes! *(She claps her hands.)* Far too lax.

Judy goes out. They get up.

Victoria	She makes Mussolini look disorganised.
Lill	Marvellous figure though.
Victoria	Shut up.

The main recreation room. Disgruntled guests are

moving about including Victoria, Lill, Connie, Enid and Sallyanne. A few people sing 'Why are we waiting?' quietly.

Connie	Why are we waiting . . .?
Enid	Why are we waiting . . .?
Lill	Will you test me on my calorie values?
Victoria	No. What's the matter with you?
Lill	I want to get thin.
Victoria	Why? Because of Marcus? He'll still be married. You'll just be hanging around, waiting in smaller trousers.
Lill	Marcus prefers petite women.
Victoria	Yes, because they're easier to tread on.

Nicola comes in.

Nicola Erm! Could I just pronounce a change of itinament? As you know, this evening's recreational fertility was to have the barndancing; but I'm afraid as of lately it has had to have been – not happening. Kirsty, who recently attended an intensive two-day Dosey Doe workshop in Lincolnshire has had to cry off for presently. She lost concentration whilst tossing a medicine ball earlier; they think the kneecap's not too bad, but they may have to splice-in a new floorboard. So as an ilternative we've decided to temporarily break our no-television Pinkney's embargo *(excited mumbles of* Eastenders *and* Bob Monkhouse *from guests)* and show a very instructative video tape featuring various slimmers; each with their own inspiring slimming story, of how they slimmed, and what it was like to slim, get slim, stay slim . . . not to be fat. *(She tails off.)* Dana! Could you wheel through now, please?

Dana, wonderfully dressed for a night out, wheels in a TV and video, and plugs it in.

Nicola So I'm sorry about the barndancing. We're still hoping tomorrow night's activity will go ahead: it's just a question of whether the blood donors' van will fit thro' the main gateway.

Dana puts in the video.

Nicola OK? Lovely. Bye!

Nicola goes out. Dana switches on the video.

Dana Right, that's me off, slaves. Going to get down the
Yellow Ferret and get boogying. *(She leaves, singing:)*
When I need you . . .

*The video begins. It's very old and poor quality from the
early 70s. Music title with logo of 'Acorn Enterprises' cuts
straight to an awful 70s girl in tank top and huge trousers
squinting into the sunlight. She speaks stiltedly.*

Girl on video Hello, I'm Melanie Dickinson, Swedacrisp Slimmer
of the Year. I used to be nineteen stone seven. You
wouldn't believe it now, would you? I can wear bikinis,
lacy feminine underwear and – yes – even hot pants.

Victoria is amused at this.

And it wasn't so hard sticking to 800 calories a day for
fourteen months – let me tell you how I did it.

Victoria nudges Lill.

Girl Lemon juice in hot water was my biggest treat . . .
Victoria Lill!
Lill *(poised with notebook and pen)* Sshh!

*Lill and Victoria's bedroom. Victoria comes in. Lill is
hopping about in a vaguely aerobic way.*

Victoria I'm so starving I've just eaten two inches of fluoride
toothpaste.
Lill That was a good tip on that slimming video, actually.
Every time you want to eat something, brush
your teeth.
Victoria If I brushed my teeth every time I wanted to eat

	something, I'd have gums up to my sinuses. Can you just stop a minute?
Lill	No I can't.
Victoria	Well it's driving me mad.
Lill	*(stopping)* Look – I've got something to tell you.
Victoria	*(apprehensively)* What?
Lill	Well, while I was here on my own I did something absolutely unforgiveable; I despise myself.
Victoria	What?
Lill	You know that squashed chocolate raisin we found in the wastepaper basket.
Victoria	Yeah?
Lill	I've been thinking about it since yesterday and as soon as you'd gone I took it out of the wastepaper basket and ate it.
Victoria	So what?
Lill	It's thirteen calories – I've been exercising since I swallowed it but I can't be sure I've burnt it all off *(jogging)*. I don't know what to do – I'll have to tell Nicola. Heaven knows what I'll weigh in the morning –
Victoria	Lill –
Lill	Marcus'll never marry me now. They'll have to wheel me into the registry office at this rate – I don't even know if they have a ramp!
Victoria	*(sitting her down)* Lill – stop it a minute. If you really want to go and tell Nicola –
Lill	I do; I have to.
Victoria	Well we'll find her in a minute. But listen – you've been going out with a married man for twelve years.
Lill	Yes.
Victoria	And some of the time you've been thin and some of the time you haven't.
Lill	Yes.
Victoria	And which ever you've been, he's never mentioned divorce.
Lill	No.
Victoria	And he has got twins and a Shetland pony.
Lill	Yes.
Victoria	So, chances are, even if you weighed less than a Pot Noodle, he'd still stay happily married.
Lill	Yes.

Victoria	And he collects beermats.
Lill	Yes. *(Pause)* I know. But I'm thirty-nine. I know I'm silly to have carried it on this long, but I kept thinking he might change his mind. If I could just flatten this and raise these.
Victoria	But if he loved you he wouldn't care, would he? You could have a bum that only just cleared the pile on an Axminster carpet and it wouldn't matter.
Lill	I know. And then I was thinking, if I did finish with him, I'd need to look good or nobody else would fancy me.
Victoria	You look good now. You can't pass a building site without some poor hunk losing his grip on the scaffolding. Come on – let's go and confess to Nicola about the chocolate raisin. Say three Hail Mary's and a Ryvita.

A corridor with the treatment room off it. Victoria and Lill pass and look through the door at Judy exercising fiercely with dumbells.

Lill	Oh but, Vic, to be all tanned and lean and disciplined like Judy.
Vic	Judy's not a person: she's worked by a computer in Milford Haven. Anyway – she's not attractive. If a man flung himself on to her in a fit of passion he'd break something.
Lill	All right – but wouldn't you like to look like Sallyanne?
Vic	No, cos then I'd have to be a topless model and stand around all day. 'Jason, can you powder my nipples?'

The recreation room. Victoria and Lill looking through a window to where a small car is parked. The strip over the windscreen reads 'Allardyce' and 'Dana'. It is rocking somewhat.

Victoria	And look at Dana – she's twice the size of you and she has a fantastic time. Dresses up, goes out, and I don't know what she's doing in the back of that car but I bet she's not working out the calories in a chocolate raisin.
Lill	You're right.

Victoria	She just has fun.
Lill	That's true, actually.
Victoria	Mind you, she's knackering the suspension.

The corridor leading to Nicola's office. Lill and Victoria are walking along.

Lill	All right – so weight's not important – but don't you think it's worth persevering with this Pinkney's regime: no caffeine, no additives, raw vegetables.
Victoria	Not with the effect they have on you. It's like sharing a room with a whoopee cushion.
Lill	Pure food, mineral water, no television.

They stop outside Nicola's door. From inside the office comes the theme music from 'Emmerdale Farm'. Lill knocks.

Nicola	*(Voice Over)* Just a memento. *(The music snaps off.)* Come through.

They go into her tiny office. Nicola is seated guiltily behind the desk, a large blank TV screen nearby.

Nicola	Can I help, ladies?
Victoria	Lill's having a fit of conscience because she's eaten a chocolate raisin and ruined her detoxification programme.
Nicola	Oh sit down.
Lill	And I do believe absolutely in everything you're trying to do here.
Nicola	What would that be?
Lill	Treating the body as a temple, pure food, no stimulants –
Nicola	Oh that.
Lill	You look marvellous on it.
Nicola	Well, to be painful, I couldn't run this healthy farm if I didn't have a few stimulants. It takes me three cups of black coffee to get my mascara on. And I don't care what they say, I like monosodium glutamate. I've got a monosodium glutamate recipe book.

Victoria	You don't eat raw broccoli?
Nicola	I can't. It has an unfortunate effect on me wind-wise. And I have to share this office.
Lill	So you don't believe in any of it?
Nicola	*(Thinks.)* I like ping-pong – *(She pauses and opens her desk drawer.)* Marshmallow?

The sauna. Connie, Enid, Lill and Victoria, all clothed, are sharing a bottle of champagne out of triangular water cups.

Lill	I never knew you'd brought a bottle of champagne in.
Victoria	You never knew about the chocolate raisins either.
Connie	*(slightly the worse for wear)* What we'll do, Lill. Lill! We'll throw a party for you – and I'll invite every man I know in Widnes.
Enid	She doesn't know any.
Connie	I figgy do, lady.
Enid	Name one.
Connie	Robin Sutherland.
Enid	In the antique shop? He'd be no use to Lill. She'd need quite a different frontal arrangement to catch *his* fancy.
Lill	Oh bother them all. Let's just have a good time.
Victoria	Hear hear.
Lill	Come on, we're going jogging.
Victoria	Oh, Lill, I thought you'd dropped all that.
Lill	We're not going far. Come on!

Night. The village street. Victoria, Connie and Enid, led by Lill, are jogging, with many complaints.

Victoria	Oh Lill!
Lill	Not much further. Onward and upward!

A small café of the egg and chip variety hoves into view. Lill leads them all towards it.

In the café. The four are standing at the counter, behind which stands a greasy man.

Lill	So that's sausage, egg and chips, sausage, beans and

chips, double egg and chips twice, four teas and four rounds of bread and butter.

Man   White or brown?

Lill   White. With additives.

Victoria   And germs on.

Four eager faces stare up at him expectantly.

The Library

The Library

Inside an Edwardian library in a large-ish town. It is open-plan, with Fiction, Children's and a Reference section, study tables, video machine etc. Pinned up with other local posters is one – 'Tape Your Memories', showing some old dear jabbering away into a tape recorder. Victoria is browsing round the shelves.

Victoria   *(to us)* This is the dreariest library in the whole world. They haven't got anything new. I think they're waiting for the Domesday Book to come out in paperback. It's run by this terrible woman called Madge, awfully narrow-minded, makes Mary Whitehouse look like a topless waitress. Never mind Salman Rushdie – she'd have the Swan Vestas to a Catherine Cookson given half a chance. She thinks book-burning is a sensible alternative to oil-fired central heating. Of course they have to order all the newspapers but if it was up to her it would just be *Nursing Mirror* and *Slimming for Nuns*. She can't bear Page Three – in fact she cuts the girls out and replaces them with a knitting pattern. Quite sad seeing all those old blokes sitting around trying to ogle a sleeveless pully.

She encounters Ted, a dirty old man, round a corner. He winks and she retreats.

Madge's taste in fiction; half of these are hospital romances – 'their eyes met over a diseased kidney' – and everything else is in large print. You try reading one with good eyesight. It's like being shouted at for three and a half hours.

She moves into Children's.

And it smells. That typical library aroma of damp

gabardine and luncheon meat. And every book's got
something scribbled in the margin – things like 'Oh I
agree', and 'We washed everything by hand too'. I mean
it's a bit disconcerting to flick through a copy of *Hamlet* to
find 'This happened to me' scrawled all over Act Four.

Madge appears from nowhere, a large frightening woman.

Madge	You know this is Children's?
Victoria	I know.
Madge	Very well. *(She leaves disapprovingly.)*
Victoria	*(crossing to reference)* She's put me off now. I was just going to squander my ticket on a nice career book: *Wendy Carstairs – Receptionist* or *Petra – Forecourt Attendant*.

*She sees Sheila, a thin anxious woman fortyish but dressed
older, being shown how to work the video by John the
nondescript fortyish assistant librarian.*

Hiyah. What are you doing?

Sheila waves her over.

John	And when you've finished, press 'Eject' and your tape comes out, and Bob's your Uncle.
Sheila	Yes he is. Thank you. I know it's a saying. But he is my uncle. Thank you.

John goes away.

Victoria	What are you doing?
Sheila	This is the new video machine.
Victoria	You can watch videos in the library? Where are they? Have they got *Petra, Forecourt Attendant – The Movie*?
Sheila	*(glancing around)* I've joined an agency.
Victoria	Have you?
Sheila	And they've sent me these videos to watch.
Victoria	What? Blue videos?

*Madge is now hanging around Ted, seated at a table,
snatching up papers and folding them with a lot of noise.*

	You'd better not watch them here. You know what Madge is like. I've seen her go through a breastfeeding manual crayonning bras on the women.
Sheila	I've made a decision, Victoria. I'm coming out of the wardrobe.
Victoria	Are you?
Sheila	Since Mother died – oh, and thank you for the flowers, we had tributes from everywhere, even the optician – I've taken stock – what do they call it? – stocktaking?
Victoria	Yeah?
Sheila	And I saw this advertisement in the post office – because I'm trying to sell my stairlift – it's in very good condition, and as I said on the postcard even if you're not disabled, it's FUN! It's called video dating. You've heard of computer dating?
Victoria	Yeah!
Sheila	Well that's gone by the roof, it's completely blasé now; so the upshot is, they send you six men on a tape and John, the assistant librarian – he used to pick me out something historical for mother – 'Bring me something where nobody dies, Sheila,' she used to say – well, that's the point of history – they're all dead – he's been through the mechanicals with me; I view the men and then contact Valerie.
Victoria	Valerie?
Sheila	She runs the agency. I've only spoken with her briefly – I had a ten pence stuck – but from the sound of her voice I think she was wearing a tie-neck blouse.
Victoria	So you pick a man?
Sheila	That's right. Well, I'm free now, it's about time I turned over a new leaf.
Victoria	Put it in then, let's have a look.
Sheila	Arrow pointing this way, and press 'PLAY'. *(Nothing happens.)* It's broken, I knew it, it's me *(pressing all buttons)*. I was the same with the spin drier – wet underskirts all over my next-door neighbour, and she's Nigerian – not much of a welcome.

The picture comes up.

*The museum tea bar. It is a small, dreary, slightly
wholefoody place. Victoria and Sheila are finishing tea.*

Victoria   I thought you said they did a good date and apple
flapjack.

Sheila   You just need to work it round your mouth a bit first.
(She roots in her bag.) Find my notes.

Victoria   Nice little book.

Sheila   Made by disadvantaged Oriental widows. You can
see here where they were too depressed to stick down
the edges.

Victoria   So who did you fancy?

Sheila   Oh I'm no judge of character, Victoria.

Victoria   Do you think *I* am? I've had my drive tarmacked
eight times.

Sheila   Give me your views on Rodney.

Victoria   Well, Rodney had white towelling socks, didn't he? Which
in my book makes him unreliable, untrustworthy and
prone to vaseline jokes. Mark . . .

Sheila   The solicitor.

Victoria   He was OK – but, as he says himself, he does a lot of
conveyancing so that'll be seventeen phone calls just to
meet him for a cup of coffee.

Sheila   I was rather taken with Simon – the gynaecologist.

Victoria   No – too inhibiting. You can't flirt with someone who can
visualise your Fallopian tubes.

Sheila   Now Malcolm – what do you think he meant by 'lively
social life'?

Victoria   Drink.

Sheila   He wants a breezy, uninhibited companion.

Victoria   To drink with.

Sheila   And what do you think he meant by 'life peppered with
personal tragedy'?

Victoria   Hangovers.

Sheila   I think you're right. He had half an Alka Seltzer stuck in
his moustache. Robert.

Victoria   Robert?

Sheila   In radiators.

Victoria   Radiators.

Sheila   The blue bri-nylon with the polo collar.

Victoria   Oh, the one with the bust! He was creepy. He looked like

	the sort of man who hangs around outside television shops watching 'Challenge Anneka' with his flies undone.
Sheila	Terry was interesting.
Victoria	Yes, wasn't he? It's not every night watchman who can wear a poncho.
Sheila	I liked him. He very much put me in mind of someone. Singer – dark curly hair – outgoing . . .
Victoria	Tom Jones?
Sheila	Alma Cogan. And Kenneth – I've put 'very rushed and jerky'.
Victoria	You had him on fast-forward.
Sheila	Well I disliked his epaulettes.
Victoria	Right.
Sheila	So that leaves Keith.
Victoria	Well he was all right, wasn't he? What did you put for him?
Sheila	Soft, sensitive, a bit woolly.
Victoria	Should be all right as long as you don't put him in the washing machine. Where are you going to meet him?
Sheila	I thought I'd do him an egg salad at home.
Victoria	Are you mad?
Sheila	Why?
Victoria	Because that's terribly dangerous.
Sheila	No, I'd boil them for twenty minutes.
Victoria	Inviting a strange man to your home: he could be an axe murderer.
Sheila	Oh no – he's got a degree in mechanical engineering.
Victoria	Meet him in a restaurant.
Sheila	*(panicking)* Oh I'm sending it back. I can't meet him anywhere. I'm no good with men – really. I can't even tackle the milkman face-to-face. I have to bob behind the ironing board and call through. And then he takes advantage. The times I've been saddled with an unrequested bilberry yoghourt.
Victoria	Meet him here for a cup of tea.
Sheila	I'll clam up, Victoria. I'm no good on my own – I clam up like – what are those things –
Victoria	Clams.
Sheila	Oysters.
Victoria	You won't – you'll be fine.
Sheila	After all those years stuck with Mother, I can't just sit

down with a man and come up with the bandage. Suppose he chucks in Giscard d'Estaing – how do I respond? I'll be stumped.

Victoria Well – do you want me to come with you?

Sheila Oh if you could just get the ball bowling – that would be marvellous.

Victoria Well I'll just stay and see that you're all right, shall I?

Sheila Mm. Just shush him out.

Victoria And if he looks like being an axe-murderer you keep him talking and I'll immobilise him with the date and apple flapjack. Yep?

The museum tea bar again, on another day. Victoria and Sheila are sitting in readiness with a tray of tea. Sheila is smartly dressed and extremely nervous.

Sheila *(suddenly)* Take off your jacket.

Victoria Eh?

Sheila It's too interesting. Take it off.

Victoria *(taking it off)* What are you worried about?

Sheila Well, as soon as he hears you're in television he's not going to squint my way, is he? He'll be querying left right and centre for insider gossip. He won't want to delve into my doings if he can get the lowdown on Patti Caldwell.

Victoria He's come to meet you.

Sheila What have I ever done? I've never even been mugged.

Victoria You've been burgled.

Sheila And what did they take? Nothing! Two apostle spoons and a bobbing bird. Robbed – I was snubbed.

Victoria Well I'll go then, shall I?

Sheila No don't – he might get the wrong idea; he might think I'm a high class call-girl.

Victoria In a museum tea room?

Sheila He may be a pervert. He may have come here specifically for the purpose of rubbing up against a scale model of Saxon Fortifications.

Victoria Well I'll stay for a few minutes.

Sheila Well, dull yourself down a bit. Set me off. Every beautiful painting needs an understated frame.

Victoria Every sizzling casserole needs an oven glove.

Sheila	He's here! I recognise his hush puppies. You pour the tea and I'll sparkle.

Keith, early middle-aged in a jacket and sweater, shirt and tie, comes in and looks around vaguely.

Victoria	He hasn't seen us – wave at him.
Sheila	I can't. I've frozen. I'm like this. I was the same with Sacha Distel in Boots. You wave.
Victoria	OK.
Sheila	Nothing too provocative or sensual.
Victoria	*(Waves awkwardly.)* Here he comes. Good luck.
Keith	Is it Sheila?
Sheila	Mmmm.
Keith	I wasn't sure if I had the correct museum.
Victoria	Would you like to sit down?
Keith	Yes I would. *(Sits slowly.)* Well I'm Keith, you're Sheila. Who's the gooseberry?
Victoria	I'm Victoria – I have to go in a minute.
Keith	Now if you were from Dewsbury, Victoria, you'd be the gooseberry from Dewsbury.
Victoria	Ah ha ha.

Keith sits quietly, pleased with this joke. Sheila pours the tea with much rattling.

Keith	When I said I was unsure as to whether I'd found the correct museum, the circumstances were these: your note, Sheila, for which much thanks, told me to expect a large building with stone pillars to my left on entering the city centre. *(Pause.)* Now would I be correct in thinking you are not familiar with the workings of the internal combustion engine?
Sheila	A with the workings, what, begging?
Victoria	You don't drive.
Sheila	Oh no. I've been shown around a tank.
Keith	And so, not being cognisant with the traffic lay-out as seen, so to speak, from the steering wheel, it will have escaped your attention that the very first building on the left is not the museum and municipal library, but the Edgar Bentley Treatment Hospital for Tropical Diseases.

Both	Ah ah.
Keith	Now, having got that off my chest, I will just equip myself with a smallish biscuit to accompany my tea and return forthwith.

Keith leaves. Significant silence.

Sheila	*He* nursed an elderly mother.
Victoria	I hope she was deaf.
Sheila	Well I don't think he's an axe-murderer.
Victoria	He doesn't need to be. Hey up.

Keith comes back in.

Keith	Well, I'm familiar with Sheila's hobbies and lifestyle as laid out in the video but what's your line of country, Vicky?
Victoria	You don't want to hear about me. Sheila's the fascinating one – she writes poems – she's a wonderful cook . . .
Keith	No – I'm an orderly fellow. Ask a question, get the reply, that's my handlebar. So, how do you rake in the shekels?
Victoria	Oh I've got such a boring job. I can hardly remember what it is.
Keith	Well let's not forget three million people in this country would *like* to be bored in that fashion.

Pause.

Victoria	I work in an office.
Keith	Now, call me a dashingly romantic sentimental old softheart, Vicky . . .
Victoria	I haven't got time.
Keith	But to me an office is more than a place of work – it's a microcosm of everyday society.
Sheila	Goodness.
Keith	What do you say to that, Vicky?
Victoria	I say – ah ha ha.
Keith	I thought so. And what office position do you hold?
Victoria	I just answer the phone.
Keith	Now therein if I may presume – we've taken tea together so we're halfway to being pals – therein

lies the cardinal error of the average telephone receptionist.

Victoria pulls a face at Sheila.

Sheila	I see in the paper today Mrs Thatcher's sporting a new brooch.
Keith	I'll ignore that, Sheila, for reasons I'll come to in a moment. The telephone receptionist of any company, be it British Telecom or Joe Bloggs of down the road Ltd, holds a unique position in the business framework. Let me clarify myself – this plate is the managing director, and this shortbread finger is the retail customer – what comes in between them?
Sheila	A doiley?
Keith	The telephone receptionist. Now take a typical day in the office . . .

Inside the library, in the video section, a few days later. Victoria and Sheila are checking their notes. Ted is reading the paper at a nearby table.

Victoria	Right – so we're going to Richard this time.
Sheila	You're sure I shouldn't persevere with Keith?
Victoria	He's boring. You've been bored for twenty years. It would be out of the frying pan into the microwave.
Madge	*(appears from afar and calls)* You two! This is not a zoo!
Victoria	So you can't help me locate the elephant house?
Madge	Quiet study or leave, please.

Madge leaves and Ted winks juicily at Victoria.

Ted	Heck of a rump on that. By cracky.
Victoria	*(more quietly)* What did we put for Richard?
Sheila	I've put 'very gentlemanly; interested in fine china and eighteenth-century English furniture. Likes visiting cathedrals, classical music; semi-retired business consultant looking for quiet, refined companion.'
Victoria	Well, you're quiet.
Sheila	Yes, but I'm not refined. I wouldn't know a Hepplewhite wotnot from a quarter of wine gums.

Victoria	It doesn't matter. Just be yourself.
Sheila	And we weren't a classical music family. If Joe 'Piano' Henderson couldn't play it we didn't hear it.
Victoria	What you want to do – is meet him for a drink and take someone really vulgar and thick with you – then you come out looking erudite and tasteful, he's bowled over and whisks you away in his Rover. What do you say?
Sheila	Well I can see the reasoning behind it – but I don't know anybody vulgar. Mother wouldn't even have our scissors sharpened because the woman had pierced ears.
Victoria	Well – meet him at the wine bar . . .

John comes in.

John	Is it working OK now?
Sheila	Yes, it wasn't irretrievably jammed, thank you, John. I had in on *pause*.
John	*(moving away)* That's good. Now, Ted, come on – no eating your sandwiches here – it's not really fair on the other readers.

Ted pretends to put them away. John leaves.

Victoria	What we'll do – you meet him at the wine bar . . .
Madge	*(coming in from nowhere)* When will you people appreciate this is an area set aside for silent study – it is not an annexe of the Millwomen and Fishwives' Debating Society.
Victoria	Sorry.
Madge	*(as she sniffs and wheels round)* You – put those sandwiches away at once. I will not have chutney on my periodicals.

Inside a quiet emptyish wine bar. Richard, a grey-haired, distinguished man in a quiet suit, sits sharing a bottle of wine with Sheila.

Richard	Well, here's to a pleasant evening.
Sheila	Yes, 'heres'.

She drinks.

Richard	I was having a quiet chuckle to myself this morning.
Sheila	Oh yes?
Richard	Radio 3 – Alicia de Larrocha with the Granados, *Quejas a la maja y el ruisenor* – very amusing interpretation. Did you catch any of it?
Sheila	No, I would probably have had on the Ken Bruce programme.
Richard	Really? *(Pause.)* I'm pleasantly surprised by the acceptability of this bouquet – are you?
Sheila	*(struggling to keep up)* Mm, I'm astounded.
Richard	Are you, as they say, 'into' wine?
Sheila	We used to make it at one time.
Richard	Really – you had a vineyard?
Sheila	We had a scullery.
Richard	*(recovering)* I should think with homemade wine one would have to be extremely patient – is that so?
Sheila	Oh yes – that's the bugbear with it – keeping your hands off the dustbin till the full ten days. *(Pause.)* Van Gogh's a very nice painter, isn't he?
Richard	I assume you're using the work in its incorrect sense – interesting.
Sheila	I love the Great Painters.
Richard	And they are . . .?
Sheila	They're a set of table mats.

Pause.

Richard	You say a friend of yours is joining us?
Sheila	Just breezing through. Here she is now actually.

Victoria comes in, a vision in skin-tight dress, tormented hair, jewellery, stilettos, the lot.

Victoria	Ooh, give us a swig of your vino, crumb-bum; I've been banging like a navvie's drill all affy.
Sheila	This is –
Victoria	Sapphire. Ciao.
Richard	Very pleased to meet you, Sapphire – I'm Richard Casey.
Victoria	He looks a bit of a Richard, dunt he, Sheila? Hey, hutch up, I'm sweating cobs. *(She sniffs her armpits.)*

Richard	May I pour you a glass, Sapphire?
Victoria	Pour us a bin bag – I'm gasping. I tell you, that window cleaner, what a snogger! I've never had such clean tonsils. And never mind a chammy – he certainly buffed up *my* corners.
Richard	And what do you do, Sapphire?
Victoria	Eh? A bit of this, bit of that, loads of the other! No, to be serious, Richard – I'm an artiste in the entertainment business. *(She fishes in her cleavage.)* Where's my card? *(She gets it out and wipes it.)* 'Miss Sapphire – Poses with a Python'. Now don't get the wrong idea – it's right artistic. Costume-wise, I never wear less than the full three tassels, and between shows I am at that python with the Dettox and a damp cloth even if he haven't been nowhere. *(She slurps her wine.)* God, I needed that – my guts! I don't care what they say on t' adverts – Malibu does not go with piccalilli. The wind I've had, Rick – I won't beat about the bungalow – I've been flatulating – and, boy, have I stunk! I mean, I don't mind for t' punters but it's not pleasant for the python. Hey – top us up, Dicky – I've got a big job on tonight. Do you ever get days, Dick when you think, 'I just do not want to thrust my groin in people's faces – I want to go home and have a go at my corns with a potato peeler.' Do you?
Richard	Well, I can't say I –
Victoria	So what do you think to our Sheila then? Eh? I mean talk about tasteful. She isn't like me; she wouldn't know a rubberised posing pouch from a sink plunger. Still – if it's a good party, who cares? *(She laughs.)*
Richard	Shall I order some more wine?
Victoria	No, I'd better push off, Rick – I've got to glue a little novelty toilet into my navel and it takes forever to dry.
Richard	Oh, no, have a little champagne before you leave. Waiter!
Victoria	All right, just a quick bottle. Now, Sheila – have you told Richard about how you're really into classical music?
Sheila	Oh yes. Ravel's 'Bolero', what a pulsing rhythm. Superb for tackling the ironing.
Richard	*(patronisingly)* And Sapphire? Any views on Ravel?
Victoria	What were he, a juggler?
Richard	*(amused)* No, a rather famous composer.
Victoria	Oh. Cos jugglers often wear boleros.

Richard	You probably know it as the Torville and Dean music.
Victoria	Weren't they a lovely couple? And they never did it. Mind you, she spent so much time lying face down on the ice, I'm not surprised.
Richard	You're not keen on the classics, then, I take it?
Victoria	Never heard of them – what are they?
Richard	Beethoven's Fifth.
Victoria	No.
Richard	Moonlight Sonata.
Victoria	Sounds like a hatchback. No.
Richard	1812 Overture.
Victoria	That rings a bell.
Richard	Daddle addle daddly dat dat dah.
Victoria	Oh yeah – my friend Suleema used to do an act to that.
Richard	What sort of an act?
Victoria	Sort of a contortionist. I won't go into details, but Christmas round her house they never needed a bottle opener, a nut cracker, or somewhere to keep the satsumas.
Richard	*(snuggling up)* This is fascinating.
Victoria	Sheila, tell Richard about your Elaine Paige records.
Richard	Elaine Paige?
Victoria	You know – blonde, titchy, goes 'Bleuh!' What a Hobsons. How they passed her over for the Royal Wedding beats me. I know she's small, but they could have stood her up on a bucket. Still, that's the Establishment for you.
Richard	You're bloody right: we're too damn stuffy about these things. God – you're refreshing.
Victoria	*(drinking, pulling a face at Sheila)* Bottoms up.
Sheila	*(leaving)* I'll just go and powder my nose.
Victoria	Don't forget to flush it!
Richard	Crikey – you're funny. So, er, what do you wear on stage exactly? Black leather boots or stilettos? Let's have the full gen.
Victoria	Er –

The library, a couple of days later; Victoria is hanging around Fiction as before.

Victoria	Sheila's given up on this video dating. She says the next time she goes out with a man, she'll be lying down with

her eyes shut and he'll be carrying the coffin. What a night with Richard. I mean when a man's on the lookout for quiet refined companionship you don't expect him to try eating pork scratchings out of your cleavage. He was dreadful in the taxi – I haven't been groped so inefficiently since I was fifteen. Once he saw me he never took another look at Sheila – good job – she finished off the champagne and was last seen in the gent's toilets flicking Quiche Lorraine over the cubicle doors.

Madge *(looming round a unit)* Are you looking for anything in particular?

Victoria I'm browsing.

Madge Well don't finger the bindings. *(She heads for the counter.)* John! What on earth are you doing with your sleeves rolled up? This isn't a massage parlour!

Sheila comes round the shelves, holding a book.

Victoria Got one?

They walk to the counter where John is being torn off a strip by Madge.

Sheila It's very difficult to find a book with no alcohol, no sex and no reference to men whatsoever.

Victoria What did you get?

Sheila *The Wincey Willis Book of Wholemeal Pasta.*

They wait to have the book stamped; Madge is still in full flow.

Madge And it isn't just your clothing, John – though heaven knows, training shoes are hardly compatible with a love of literature. It's your wishy-washy liberal attitude – video machines and Asian novels here, taped reminiscences there – mark my words, John, make people welcome in the library and it's the thin end of the bookmark; before you can say 'Monica Dickens' they'll be drying their underwear on the radiators and doing boil-in-the-bag noodles behind the photocopier. Kindly digest. If anybody wants me I shall be in

the stacks with a Jackie Collins and a felt-tip pen.
She leaves.

John Just the one book, Sheila? Er – sorry about that –
Sheila Oh, she doesn't bamboozle me. I remember her when she first came – never seen so many kirbys in a French pleat.
John Cookery book, eh? Now that's my absolute blind spot, I'm afraid. I really am clueless.
Sheila Oh I'm nuts on cuisine. I really miss having somebody to cook for. There's a lovely thing in here with courgettes but it's not worth doing for one.
John Well, if you ever need an extra mouth . . .
Sheila Well I was thinking of doing a little meal this evening if you've no plans afoot?
John No, I haven't but –
Victoria Sheila!
Sheila I'm not being forward, Victoria. I like to think of myself as liberated – I could have burnt my bra but it was long-line and I didn't have the time. So would you care to accept my invitation to dinner?
John Certainly – and I very much appreciate it.
Sheila Eight o'clock then. Bye.

They leave.

Victoria You didn't give him your address.
Sheila He's a librarian. He'd find it sharp enough if I owed 8p on a Georgette Heyer.

Victoria and Sheila are walking along a quiet street of semis.

Victoria Just have somebody in the house with you – that's all I'm saying. Haven't you got an Auntie Lill or a Cousin Ida?
Sheila I've got an Auntie Lill *and* a Cousin Ida. One's in Toronto and the other's body-building in Hendon.

They stop outside the house.

Victiria Well, shall I do it?
Sheila Oh no, we've had the last twice.

Victoria	I'll hide in the garden – keep an eye through the window.
Sheila	You can't, we've got vigilantes. Mr Brewer's forever up and down the avenue with a beret and a ping-pong bat.
Victoria	*(striding up the path)* I know! Come on!
Sheila	Hang on – my Yale's under my Wincey Willis.

Sheila's house. The hall, stairs, and bathroom door at the top of the stairs. All is clean and neat and ten years out of date. Sheila stands anxiously outside the bathroom door.

Sheila	Are you nearly ready?
Victoria	*(Voice Over)* Yeah, I won't be a sec. Now, you know the plan?
Sheila	I take him in the kitchen, introduce you, explain you won't be joining us for dinner then take him through into the dining room.
Victoria	*(Voice Over)* And I'll be in the kitchen the whole time so just give us a shout if he gets frisky.
Sheila	If he gets what?
Victoria	*(Voice Over)* Frisky!
Sheila	*(pattering down the stairs)* Will do! I thought you said frisky!

Victoria's puzzled face appears round the door.

Sheila's hall. She opens the front door to a nervous John.

Sheila	Oh, come in.

He trips.

	Mind the mat. It's from the Philippines – and I'm not sure they always take quite the trouble.
John	Well it's rather a corrupt society.
Sheila	Oh I know. Take your coat off. I saw a documentary. It looked to be quite an uprising, even with the sound off.
John	*(standing by the coat stand)* Shall I? *(He hangs coat on a knob.)*
Sheila	Yes do. *(All the coats fall down.)* Oh, that coatstand. I arranged to have it renovated but they lost interest when they heard it was just a knob.

John	I could probably glue it back on for you.
Sheila	Oh could you?
John	If you have any glue, perhaps after dinner –
Sheila	I may have some UHU left over from the Nativity. Anyway – come through to the kitchen . . .

Inside Sheila's kitchen. It is clean but dreary; lots of pots and pans are bubbling away. Victoria is at the kitchen table in old lady dress and woolly hat. Sheila and John come in.

Sheila	This is my auntie *(she casts around the room)* Marjoram – Marjorie.
John	I'm very pleased to meet you.
Victoria	'Appen as mebbe. But you'll know what they say?
John	No, what's that?
Victoria	Pleased to meet is sorry to greet come Michaelmas.
John	Now, I've never heard that; isn't that fascinating!
Victoria	Now you don't want to waste your time with an old outhouse like misen – get the knees under t' table and set to supping.
John	You're not joining us for dinner then, Mrs – ?
Victoria	Witherstrop. Nay – I topped up long since. Nice plate of brains and a ginger nut. Tek him through, Sheila – I shall be all right here.
Sheila	Right – John – ?
John	*(sitting down)* I'm sure there's time for a little chat, Sheila?
Victoria	Oh, no, you get about your dining arrangements. Them as chat shall never grow fat.
John	That's another lovely saying I've never come across.
Sheila	*(at the stove)* I'll just finish off if you're all right, John?
John	Certainly. Gosh, it's warm in here. Can I take your hat, Mrs Withersdrop?
Victoria	I can't tek it off, lad. I lost every hair on my head the day they bombed Eccles.
John	Blast.
Victoria	That's what I said.
Sheila	I'm sure John doesn't want to hear about that, Marjorie.
John	No, I'd love to.
Victoria	February the eleventh, 1941. I was clocking off from work – aye, from munitions – they had to convert when war

broke out – they had been making liquorice torpedoes
so it weren't too much of an upheaval. Vera Lynn were
coming over the Gannex –

John   I beg your pardon?

Victoria   The tannoy. Big Ellen Mottershead turned to me – her
crossover pinnie was wet with tears. 'It's a bomber's
moon, Marjorie,' she said, 'It's a bomber's moon.'

John   Look – I'm sorry to interrupt – this is absolutely
fascinating and just what I need.

Victoria   Eh?

John   My taped reminiscence programme – it's been very hard
to get it off the ground – a lot of opposition from Madge.
These stories of yours are just what I need to get the ball
rolling. Sheila – would you mind if I just fetched my tape
recorder?

Sheila   No.

John   I won't be one sec.

He dashes out of the back door.

Sheila   I thought you said no one could possibly have an interest
in an old woman. What a marvellous evening I'm going
to have.

Victoria   Well, I'll keep it short.

Sheila   How? He wants your life story.

Victoria   I'll tell him I was killed in an air raid.

John reappears with a tape recorder.

John   Actually, Mrs Withersdrop, I've been thinking – it's
awfully rude to suddenly conduct an interview with you
when Sheila has this lovely meal already prepared.

Victoria   Aye, well.

John   So what I thought was, rather than me bombarding you
with questions, if Sheila doesn't mind, my uncle's in the
car outside – if he could perhaps come in, I'll set the
machine going and you could both chat together, I should
think you're pretty much of an age.

Sheila   Bring him in, by all means.

John   *(shouting from the doorway)* Uncle Ted! Come
in then!

Sheila	But what's he doing in the car? I don't follow.
John	Well I'm sure you'll think I'm a bit of a weed – but you read such terrible things in the papers; men kidnapped by fanatical women, used as sex slaves – I brought Ted as a safety precaution.
Sheila	I wouldn't kidnap a man for sex – I'm not saying I couldn't use someone to oil the mower.

Ted comes in.

Ted	Hey up, fans!
John	This is Mrs Withersdrop, Ted. She's going to tape her memories of the raid on Eccles.
Ted	*(sitting down)* There never were a ruddy raid on Eccles – there were nowt worth bombing, bar two tarts at the bus station.
Victoria	Aye, well – my memory's not what it was.
John	Well I'll just leave the tape running – you two settle down and have a really good chat about the old days and Sheila and I can get stuck into our dinner.
Sheila	Lovely. If you'll just push the trolley, John.

John goes out with the laden trolley.

Offer Ted a beer, Marjorie – you may be in for a long evening.

Sheila leaves with a bottle of wine. Victoria snaps open a beer for Ted. He slurps and belches.

Ted	Pardon.
Victoria	Right, well, let's get it over with. I was born in a one up one down. My mother washed everything by hand, and I didn't set eyes on a sprout till I was seventeen.

Ted switches off the tape.

Ted	Never mind John's old rubbish. *(He hutches his chair up and lays a heavy hand on her leg.)* By! That's a leg

and a half. I tell you what – I may be seventy-eight but
I've still plenty of snap in my celery. You know what
they say?

Victoria   What?

Ted   There's many a new piston under an old bonnet.

We'd Quite Like To Apologise

We'd Quite Like To Apologise

A motorway with a long shot of non-moving traffic.

Radio Jingle	Travel News.
David Jacobs	*(Voice Over)* And because of that earlier incident, traffic is still tailing back from the airport turn-off for several miles. Police advise motorists to keep calm and on no account to erect sun loungers on the hard shoulder . . .

Inside Victoria's car. There is a banana skin on the passenger seat.

David Jacobs	*(Voice Over)* Well if you are stuck in that jam, and I hope to goodness you're not . . .
Victoria	I am, thank you, David.
David Jacobs	*(Voice Over)* Why not sit back and relax to the velvety tones of Jack Jones as he tries to find the way, not to the airport but to Amarillo.

Victoria snaps the button to Radio One.

Gary Davies	*(Voice Over)* Good good. So you play golf?
Young male Contestant	*(Voice Over)* Pardon, Gary?
Gary Davies	*(Voice Over)* You play a bit of golf, Paul?
Paul	*(Voice Over)* What's that, sorry?
Gary	*(Voice Over)* The game with the clubs.
Paul	*(Voice Over)* Yeah, I go to the clubs, Gary.
Gary	*(Voice Over)* But you don't actually play golf?
Paul	*(Voice Over)* Not with you, Gary.

Victoria changes to Radio Four and the sound effect of a car not starting.

Nigel	*(Voice Over)* It's no use, Shulie – that organic

yoghurt is marvellous stuff but I don't think putting it in the petrol tank was a terribly good idea.

Shula *(Voice Over)* Oh, Nigel – what are we going to do? It was bad enough being caught half naked in Felpersham Cathedral, but if I'm not on the Borchester By-Pass in fifteen minutes I'm jolly well going to miss that plane!

Archers' theme.

Victoria switches off radio, looks at watch and sighs.

Inside the airport multi-storey short stay car park. Two queues of cars are going in to park, one moving reasonably quickly, the other, with Victoria's as the third car, stationary. Inside Victoria's car there are now five banana skins on the passenger seat. She is peering agonisedly out of window at old buffer at head of queue gazing out of his car window at the ticket machine.

Victoria Press the button and take the ticket, you dithering old pillock.

He does so and the car moves forward.

And stop being so BALD!

The woman in the heading car looks at the ticket machine. She turns to her passenger.

Victoria Hurry up!

The woman peers at the machine again.

It's a ticket machine – get a blinking ticket out of it!

The woman gets out of her car. She puts on glasses, which are on a chain round her neck, and peers even closer.

Victoria	Stop looking at it. It's not a Henry Moore.
	She gets out of the car and approaches the woman.
Victoria	What's happening? This is a ticket machine. Are you looking for a sell-by-date?
Woman	I was just trying to see what –
Victoria	What this says? It says 'manufactured 1987 by Denby Ticket Machines Ltd, Ticket Machine House, Didsbury'. This says 'Press for Ticket'. Press for Ticket. Take Ticket. Get in car. Find Space. Park. Get on plane. Go on holiday. Sunbathe. Drink.

She leads the woman back into her car and slams the door.

Have sexual intercourse with Portuguese Timeshare salesman. But first get in the car and move!

The woman moves off and Victoria goes back to her car. A hoot from car behind.

Hello!

Victoria's car winds quickly and none too accurately up and up and up to the only space. Victoria gets out of her car, locks it, and runs in the direction of the lift.

Inside the lift. Victoria dashes in. Another woman is holding the doors open.

Victoria	Thanks.

The woman continues to hold the doors open. Victoria looks at her.

Woman	My husband's just coming.
Victoria	*(Pause.)* Where from – Bangladesh?

She looks at her watch and dashes out of the lift, side-stepping a man with trolley piled high. She runs along

a corridor, then pounds along the travelator. She
stops for breath, checks her watch, relaxes slightly.
She smiles at a second man surrounded by cases.

Second man	Don't suppose I'll need half this luggage.
Victoria	Luggage –

She suddenly turns round and dashes madly the
wrong way up the travelator.

Victoria	Hold the lift!

Inside the airport is a main hall with check-in desks.
Victoria appears at the far end with baggage and
makes one last dash to the 'Sunflight' desk furthest
away. She leans against the desk, shattered.

Victoria	Alicante – am I in time?
Girl	Well, we do like people to check in two hours in advance of flying.
Victoria	I know – I'm sorry. It was the traffic.
Girl	To be explanatory – you have ample minutage because your flight is carrying a small delay.
Victoria	Oh that's great *(She puts her bags on the scale.)*
Girl	You're just on your kilo limit – so if you're bringing back souvenirs you will have to leave something else behind. Current rate of exchange is one ashtray to three bikini briefs – that's for a normal smoker and a twelve to fourteen hip.
Victoria	How long's the delay?
Girl	Not too distressing. Just the four or five hours.
Victoria	Oh great – sorry – hours?
Girl	Four or five – we're pending on a definite there. Or six. They're fairly confident it won't balloon to seven. Talking or non-talking?
Victoria	Talking.
Girl	Any particular seat? *(She turns to a plan.)* This one has toilet access. This one has apricot jam on the armrest and this has restricted view of the movie.
Victoria	What is the movie?
Girl	*Police Academy Nine.*

Victoria	I'll sit there. And I asked for a vegetarian meal.
Girl	That's right.
Victoria	So will I be getting that?
Girl	No.
Victoria	Oh.
Girl	To be almost direct – there have been inadequacies re in-flight cuisine. Our Clipper Club Business Members have been particularly vocal over the breakfasts. As they say – how can they shuttle on a bran muffin? They're very dissatisfied cum hygiene.
Victoria	Are they?
Girl	In fact, one particular gentleman was so dissatisfied he died. The problem is, so many journalists have infiltrated the catering side to expose airport security, your lunch is probably being cobbled together by two feature writers from the *Independent*. Enjoy your flight – should there be one.
Victoria	Thanks.

Inside the airport's main concourse café. Victoria is seated at a table.

Victoria	*(to us)* Three hours I've been here now. There's nothing to do. I've been in the Sock Shop seventeen times. I've bought something in the Body Shop, the Tie Rack and Knickerbox. I'm so brainwashed I went in the Ladies and said how much are your soap dispensers? I've read *Woman, Woman's Own, Woman's Realm, Woman's Weekly* and *Boxer Shorts Bulletin*. My free gifts have included a bronzy pink lipgloss, a muesli bar and a macaroni effect toast enhancer.

I've done three quizzes to put me in touch with myself, and now realise I'm too agoraphobic to leave the country; I should be working with my hands and wearing navy. I've just spent £16.52 on a glass of water and a salad sandwich that took me twenty minutes to open because it was double shrink wrapped to avoid tampering. When I did get it open it was so boring I took it back to the counter and asked if someone could tamper with it.

I've eaten so much chocolate: I've had the chocolates that melt in your mouth and not in your hand. I've had the chocolates that don't melt in your mouth and get stuck in your fillings. And I particularly enjoyed the chocolates that melt in your handbag without ruining your appetite. Do you think I've missed an announcement? Do you think while I'm sitting here everyone else is doing the Birdy Song up and down Alicante high street?

Do you think my luggage is being picked over by Spanish lavatory attendants? 'Don't think much to her sponge bag do you, Concepcion?' *(She taps her fingers, and looks at her watch.)* I've only come away to relax. Everything's getting on top of me. I can't switch off. I've got a self-cleaning oven – I have to get up in the night to see if it's doing it.
I worry about the ice caps melting. Some tropical islands are going to be submerged altogether. As it is, where we live we stand to lose a bit of privet and a bird table. People tell me worry beads are good. Suppose they break and somebody trips on them? *(She gets up.)* Somebody must know something.

The 'SunSeaKing' information desk; just a little counter and chair, unattended. Victoria is hanging around it. Una comes up, a small worried woman in her fifties.

Una	Oh dear – is there nobody here?
Victoria	No.
Una	I don't know what's happened to SunSeaKing. Last year they couldn't have been more helpful. We were only delayed ten minutes and they were in there handing out colouring books. Are you 603 for Alicante?
Victoria	Yes.
Una	Isn't it terrible? I feel like going home, I really do. I'd leave now but I've promised to deliver a walking frame.

Victoria	Have you?
Una	You can't obtain them there. Well they're such a proud peoples – I think they prefer to limp. I thought you were on my flight. I spotted your labels in the Sky Shop. I was seeing if they had anything fizzy for malaria. Are you staying at the Casa D'Oro?
Victoria	Yes.
Una	I go every year. Marvellous. The only hotel on the Costa Blanca to serve Bengers.
Victoria	It's not all English food is it?
Una	Oh no – I've very happy memories of their Scotch pancakes. They do have a Spanish menu but I have to think twice, having only half a colon.
Victoria	A semi-colon.
Una	I wouldn't normally toss my bowels into the conversation this early but I'm travelling alone and it pays to be open. I did advertise for a holiday companion – capable widow, no sense of humour, some knowledge of haemorrhoids preferred – not a reply.
Victoria	Really?
Una	That's Eastbourne for you. I mean, it's cheaper with two isn't it? Somebody to go halves on the verucca tablets. Perhaps we could chum up.
Victoria	Mm.
Una	Stick with me and you may never have to speak to a Spaniard the whole fortnight. I do think somebody ought to come and tell us what's happening. Is there nothing behind there – a message or –
Victoria	*(going behind the desk)* There's a half-eaten packet of Cheese Murmurs – would you like one?
Una	Not when I'm tense. That sort of savoury niblet sets my ulcer hopping like a ping-pong ball.

John and Barbara come in. She is downtrodden and carrying all the hand luggage. He is fuming, middle-aged. He approaches the desk and addresses Victoria.

John	Now look – we have been here since 10.15 this morning. We had a heck of a drive from Knutsford

– the windscreen washers packed up and my wife spent the last fifty miles hanging out of the sunroof, picking flies off as and when they landed. We've been here for eight hours with nothing to do but buy socks and, quite frankly, it's not adequate enough. There's been no apologies, no information. Good Golly – the delays with Summerbird last year were marvellous: Bingo, Community Singing – we were sorry to leave and go on our holidays. What's going on, is my question quite simply – don't fob me off with flannel. I'm in contract carpeting and in contract carpeting, we carpet first, flannel later. So – and my wife is witnessing this – what is your name, what position do you hold in this company, and why do you not have the common courtesy to be wearing a uniform? Well?

Victoria   OK – my name's Victoria, the position I hold is holidaymaker, I do have a uniform; it is very small, very brown and if I was wearing it I would do this and dance round a toadstool.

John   Point taken. No offence. I laid my carpet there without preparing my floorboards. John Appleby.

Victoria sits down.

Una   We're waiting for news as well. Isn't it dreadful? I wish I'd given Spain a miss this year – I nearly plumped for a crochet week in Rhyl. I was going to have a stab at a batwing blouson.

Barbara   I'll ring this bell, shall I?

John   You'll be lucky. Good griffin, they can put a man on the moon, microwave ovens . . .

Una   Oh, not the hard floor. That's how mine started. Haven't had peace in the powder room since.

John   *(half to himself)* It beats me – we've got silicon chips, videos . . .

Barbara   I think someone's coming now.

In comes Joyanne, tanned, in her thirties, lots of jewellery, and denim jacket with diamante; a professional girlfriend.

Joyanne	Are you flying to Alicante?
John	Trying to. Good goblins – we've got non-stick pans, weathermen . . .
Joyanne	Have they said how much longer it's going to be?
Victoria	There's nobody here.
Barbara	We've rung the bell.
Una	And that was what – half a minute ago?
Joyanne	Tuh. The first two or three hours I didn't mind, because I was choosing stockings but this – honestly – *(She looks at a tiny watch)* talk about retarded!
Una	I don't mind waiting for myself, but it's my intestines –

Kathy comes in, a friendly, pleasant girl in her mid-twenties.

Kathy	Is this the SunSeaKing desk?
John	Supposed to be, Good Gordon!
Una	We're waiting for someone to come.
Barbara	I've rung the bell.
Una	And that was what – just over a minute ago?
Kathy	And nobody's come?
John	Need you ask? I don't know, we've got Thermos flasks, air fresheners . . .
Kathy	*(calling)* Alan! Over here! Everyone's over here!

Alan comes in, a nice young man. They kiss.

Kathy	Missed you.
Alan	Missed *you*. So – what's happening?
Kathy	They're waiting for someone to come.
Barbara	I've pressed the bell.
Una	That's about a minute and a quarter ago now, I should think.
Joyanne	Well you'd rung it before I got here, hadn't you?
Una	That's right.
Alan	And has nobody come?
Kathy	That's what I said – telepathic!
Alan	Love you.
Kathy	Ditto.

Victoria is getting more and more fed up as this goes on.

Una	Nobody's come so far.
Joyanne	Three hours.
Barbara	It's getting ridiculous.
Joyanne	Well it's more than ridiculous really, it's silly.
John	When you think we've got satellites, vitamins, shower curtains . . .
Una	I mean, no one minds waiting for a limited period.
Joyanne	Or even a bit longer than that.
Kathy	We bought a pair of socks, didn't we, Alan?
Barbara	I must say this airport is very good for socks.
John	Button it, Barbara, for heaven's sake.
Alan	So, sorry, can I just recap on the situation?
Kathy	I love the way you say 'situation'.
Alan	The bell's been pressed?
Una	Yes, this lady pressed it – I would say over two minutes ago.
Alan	But nobody's come?
Una	To be fair, nobody's come 'as yet'.
John	Talk about Waiting for Godot.
Joyanne	At least Godot turned up. *(She thinks.)* Or was that Hamlet? One of those books anyway.

Guy, a sprightly young man in airline uniform (not SunSeaKing) crosses behind the desk.

Victoria	Excuse me?
Guy	*(rather offhand)* Yes?
Victoria	Do you know anything about the delay on the Alicante flight?
Guy	No – is it very exciting?
Alan	Perhaps we should start at the beginning.
Barbara	I saw the bell and I though I should press it.
Una	We'd seen it previously but hadn't gone as far as to ring it.
Joyanne	When I got here – that had already happened.
Kathy	And we arrived bang in the middle – didn't we, Alan?

Guy	*(to Victoria)* Where do you fit in?
Victoria	I'm the understudy. If anybody drops out I'll be right in there – I know all the lines.
Guy	Well I'm sorry, you'll just have to carry on waiting.
Barbara	Carry on waiting – sounds like a 'Carry On' film.
Una	*(to Barbara)* Like *Carry on Camping*.
Joyanne	*(to Una) Carry on Nurse*.
Alan	*(to Kathy) Carry on Doctor*.
Kathy	*(to Alan) Doctor in the House*.
Victoria	Could you maybe find out what's happening? We've been here ages.
Joyanne	Two or three hours you don't mind –
Victoria	*(through gritted teeth)* Thank you, would you mind?

Guy sits down at the desk and picks up the phone.

Guy	Mm – Cheese Murmurs – aren't they more-ish? Si? It's Guy. Hi. *(Pulling his eyelid back and rolling his eye up)* Beg pard? No, I'm just fiddling with my contact lens. Oh I'm glad you enjoyed it – it wasn't a bad moussaka for a first attempt, was it? *(He laughs.)* No, I put Daz on it – it came out no trouble. *(He laughs, then stops.)* Anyway, Si, SunSeaKing 603 Alicante – any joy? Yeah, yeah, OK, all right – I'll see you there – and don't forget the dry ginger – take it easy!

He puts the phone down, and reverts to his off-handedness.

	You were right.
Victoria	What?
Guy	It's delayed.
Victoria	What shall we do?
Guy	We usually advise people in this situation to mill aimlessly about.
Una	Is that all?
Guy	You could always buy socks. I should check with your SunSeaKing representative.
Una	She's not here.

Guy	*(looking blankly around)* Oh. *(He strolls away.)* Ring the bell, I would. Take it easy.
Una	Well at least we know where we stand – we're not just late – it is a delay.
John	Well I'm going to find the head honcho. This is an abomination. To put it in carpeting terms, we've been here five hours and we haven't even got our gripper-rods down.
Kathy	If we don't get there tonight I'm going to have a sun top left over.
Alan	Oh darling, which one?
Kathy	The little white strappy one with the anchor.
Alan	How rotten, darling.
Joyanne	Perhaps we should ring the bell again.
Una	Well it has been rung twice.
Barbara	Yes, because I pressed it originally.
Una	And we're going back about four minutes now.
Victoria	Look!

Flying towards them, bright and breezy, is the 'SunSeaKing' girl, Carol. General relief all round. She is very cheerful, fluffs her hair, and plonks clipboard down on desk.

Carol	Hi! I'm Carol, your SunSeaKing representative. I'm flying out to replace Donna – she's still in hospital, she had an accident, she fell off an architect. Are you all for Alicante?

General murmurs of 'Yes, if we ever get there' etc.

Una	*(out of the general chat)* Hope we don't have to wait another five hours.
Carol	*(blankly)* Five hours?
John	We were supposed to leave at two.
Carol	Were we? *(She checks her clipboard.)* I could have sworn that was a seven! *(She laughs.)* Good job it was delayed – I'd have missed it altogether. *(She laughs again.)* Oh – so – how long is it delayed for?
Alan	We thought you would know.
Carol	Me? I've been at the hairdressers.

Victoria	Well, anyway, what do we do now?
Carol	I'm not really sure – have you tried ringing this bell?

At the departure gate. There are seats, tables, and a small snack bar. All the company met so far plus a few extras are sitting down, waiting. Victoria is next to Kathy; Alan brings over teas.

Alan	I missed that – what was it?
Victoria	Thanks.
Kathy	I was telling Victoria how we adopted Keith last year on holiday.
Alan	That's right. We don't like to see anybody lonely.
Kathy	He said he was a loner. He said he was quite happy on his own. I said, 'Keith – you're coming with us.'
Alan	And we never let him out of our sight the whole fortnight, did we?
Kathy	No; wherever he went, we found him. He could be all on his own sunbathing or having a quiet drink –
Alan	And we'd pop up – go 'Boo!'
Kathy	Drop a few ice cubes down his swimming trunks – do a bit of a prank on him . . .
Alan	Sometimes he'd say, 'Kathy and Alan will you please leave me alone,' and he'd even get quite irritated.
Kathy	But he wasn't – he needed us. Funny – the last night of the holidays – we'd been with him all day helping him windsurf – come the Fancy Dress Barbecue, we couldn't find him anywhere.
Alan	Room was empty –
Kathy	They found his clothes in a little pile on the beach, but of Keith – no sign. Funny . . . but it makes our holiday having someone to look after.
Alan	Course you're here on your own, Victoria, aren't you?
Victoria	Yes.

Carol rushes in.

Carol	My fault everybody! When I said, 'Please proceed to the gate the plane is on the tarmac,' apparently it was on the tarmac, but not our tarmac, it was on

some other tarmac – in Belgium. But it is on the way
now. Please help yourself to drinks and refreshments
– it's all courtesy of SunSeaKing holidays –
thank you.

*Later in the day. Everyone is more dishevelled; all
have changed around; there is more litter on the
tables. Joyanne and Victoria are now together, Kathy
and Alan nearby, whispering sweet nothings.*

Joyanne	What are you reading?
Victoria	Evelyn Waugh.
Joyanne	Is she good? *(Pause.)* I wouldn't have thought she'd have time with her problem page. I've brought a book – oh what's it called? It's got a little penguin on the cover – it's just one big word.
Victoria	*Lace – Scruples?*
Joyanne	*Groin!* Have you read it?
Victoria	No is it good?
Joyanne	Yes it is, actually, because it's not just sex, there's quite a lot of literature in it as well.

She thrusts her wrist in Victoria's face.

	Gorgeous, isn't it? It's nothing in the bottle, but on the nipple it's fabulous. *(Pause.)* Is someone paying for this holiday for you?
Victoria	No I'm paying for it.
Joyanne	Now that's silly, Victoria – and I'll tell you for why. The more you get them to pay for, the more they respect you. I have three serious boyfriends, OK – Malcolm pays my mortgage; Mustapha's furnished my maisonette right through to the fixtures and Tony – well, you name it with Tony – rebounder, sheepskin jacket, dogfood – he's very much the gentleman is Tony.
Victoria	Doesn't Malcolm mind about Tony – or –
Joyanne	My motto is very much, you don't have to be ugly to be a woman's libber. I don't go along with everything they wear, don't get me mistaken, but if I want three boyfriends and perhaps a couple of carnal

relationships ditto to that – well, *vive la France.* And
the good thing about the Casa D'Oro is it's next to
the Hotel Golf and that's where you find a lot of
trousers with nothing to spend their money on. Do
you like Scotch?

Victoria No.

Joyanne I came back with a bottle *that* big, three silk blouses
and a pair of court shoes and I was only there five
days. So what say I pick you up tomorrow evening,
nine-ish? *(She starts looking through her handbag.)*

Victoria Sorry?

Joyanne All right, nine-thirty. Nice and glam though, yes?
(She laughs.) I can see you're like me, Vicki, when
you're travelling, any old rags will do!

She gets a photo out of her bag. Carol comes in.

Carol Well, it's good news and bad news I'm afraid.
(Groans.) The bad news is our plane has lost its
place in the queue and the pilot's having to circle
for half an hour or so before he can land. *(More
groans.)*

Victoria What's the good news?

Carol It's my birthday tomorrow.

*She escapes amidst boos and paper cups being
thrown etc.*

Joyanne These are my curtains, Victoria. This is my
wallpaper. Real leather. Mustapha's family are *in*
leather . . . And these are my banisters . . .

*The same, later. Chairs have been pushed into a
circle – all are entertaining each other. Una has a
joke book.*

Una I'll just read one more and then somebody else can
have a go. Right. Victoria – why did the chicken
cross the road?

Victoria It saw two Mormons coming out of Woolworths?

Una *(seriously)* Hang on. *(Drops book.)* What

	page were we on? Elephant jokes – we've had all those.
Victoria	All those.
Barbara	*(having had far too much wine)* Well, it's my turn to entertain everybody.
John	Pipe down, Ba.
Barbara	No I will not pipe down, John! He thinks I can't do anything. When he was in ceiling tiles he used to look up to me, but now he's in contract carpeting he treats me like underlay.
John	My wife's a little bit tired I think.
Barbara	Yes; I'm a little bit tired of you!
John	When did this all start?
Barbara	The second night of our honeymoon if you must twig. I was upstairs in a slit-sided *peignoir* – he was in the TV lounge glued to 'Sunday at the London Palladium'.
John	Only till 'Beat the Clock'.
Barbara	Twenty-seven years I've suffered in silence – matches in every fireplace – never a lavatory seat down when you want one –
Victoria	Shame.
John	Don't you assist.
Barbara	She understands. Not everyone's an unthinking barbarian like you. The things I could tell you, Victoria. His underwear habits alone would baffle a psychiatrist –

Carol comes in.

| **Carol** | All right everybody – we're ready for take-off. |

Cheers and general packing up.

So if you'd like to get on the bus . . .

Moans and grumbling.

And to really get us into the SunSeaKing holiday atmosphere – all together *(singing)* 'One man went to mow, went to mow a meadow . . .'

She carries on singing and gradually everyone joins in as they shuffle to the door.

Inside a small airport bus, Victoria is jammed into a man's armpit. Standing. The song continues – 'Seventeen, sixteen, fifteen' etc.

Carol (*Voice Over*) We think we've located the correct runway, folks, so not long now.

Victoria *(to us)* I don't mind the man that goes to mow and I'm not too fussed about the meadow – but the thing that really gets on my wick is the dog. *(Voices – 'And his dog, Spot'.)* In this case – Spot. I can't believe he's any help mowing the meadow can you? Spot – doesn't sound very reliable to me. I can just see him panicking and getting caught up in the combine harvester. And it would give the whole song a lift – cos God knows the suspense factor is nil – if it went 'five men four men three men' – I may not have the lyrics quite right – 'three men, two men, one man and his dog – oops – fell into the mower', like ten green bottles, wouldn't that be improved if the wall fell down and the bottles stayed up there?

The bus lurches Victoria up against armpit.

Now if I'd travelled as a VIP it wouldn't be like this. I wouldn't have my nose up an armpit from start to finish – well, only from choice. I'd have been in the celebrity lounge at Heathrow now, sipping herb tea and reaching past Anne Diamond for the Twiglets. Don't tell me Jason Donovan and Kylie Minogue sit there singing 'One Man Went to Mow' – it's a little bit of a profound concept for one of their songs. I shouldn't have come on a package – I should have been adventurous, struck out, pushed mind and body to the limit: freezing water, primitive people, strange food – but Butlins isn't like that anymore apparently. Even my next-door neighbours went to Brazil, brought back some lovely souvenirs;

woodcarvings, wallhangings – twins. I don't know what they'll do when they get too big for the bay window. The only good thing is, I'm not at the Casa D'Oro itself – I'm in the annexe. Self-catering, so with any luck I won't have to see any of those upsetting misfits ever again.

The bus jerks to a halt and Victoria is crushed up against armpit.

Doing his bit for the ozone layer.

Inside the plane. Victoria sits next to Una, Joyanne and Barbara across the aisle. Behind Victoria are Kathy and Alan. They all have their hand luggage on their knees.

Una	I've left my joke book behind.
Victoria	Never mind.
Una	*(anxiously)* Yes, but I keep thinking – why *did* that chicken cross the road? What was on its mind?
Pilot	*(Voice Over)* I'd like to take this opportunity to welcome you all aboard flight 603 to Alicante. We hope to take off as soon as possible – just a couple of procedures to be gone through first. I'm waiting for clearance and I also have a couple of egg sandwiches to finish.

Carol stops by Victoria with a clipboard.

Carol	May as well save time at the other end by running through room allocations, excursion and so on and *et cetera*. Now I'll give you all your vouchers now – this is for tonight on arrival – in reception, 'Punch and Pudding Party'.
Victoria	Pudding?
Carol	Yorkshire pudding. So one for you, Joyanne, Una and here's yours –
Victoria	I don't need one: I'm not in the hotel – I'm self-catering in the annexe.

Una	Oh that looked lovely in the brochure – artist's impression.
Carol	*(laughing)* It's like that terrible Spanish holiday joke: looked good in the brochure, hasn't been built yet.
Victoria	How do you mean?
Carol	It hasn't been built yct. You're in the hotel, block seven, segment W.
Una	That's my segment!
Carol	Well we thought rather than pay the supplement you could share a room with Una – you've got Kathy and Alan on one side, Barbara and John on the other, and Joyanne just across the way, so you'll be able to join in all the fun.
Una	Is there a donkey excursion this year?
Carol	I believe so. *(She reads.)* Yes, 'Leisurely ramble through the geranium-filled winding lanes ending up at Miguel's Mini Mart and Paella Parlour'. A burger and bun comes *with* that.
Victoria	I think I'll give that one a miss.
Kathy	Put her name down, Carol! Alan and I will get her on that donkey or our name's not Warburton.
Victoria	Is their name Warburton?
Una	Yes.
Victoria	Oh.
Carol	I'll leave you the list, shall I?

Victoria reads, each one is greeted by enthusiastic cries.

Victoria	Raffia Demonstration. Tour of castanet factory. Wicker donkey weaving and charcoal grill. Poolside limbo and sombrero parade. Winetasting and Flamenco night.
Una	Does a burger and bun come with that too?
Victoria	No, just a bucket and a damp cloth.

Bing Bong from P.A.

Pilot	*(Voice Over)* Captain Lewis speaking again, I'm afraid. You'll be glad to hear I've finished my sandwiches – I'll have the apple and the wafer biscuit

once we get going. Now there's nothing to worry about, but a little warning light has appeared on the dashboard here –

Victoria *(to camera)* Dashboard?

Pilot *(Voice Over)* Probably means nothing at all, but it's prudent not to leave until we've located the source of the problem. I'm afraid we can't offer you any drinks while we're waiting, but the flight attendants will be circulating with a tray of objects which you're welcome to memorise.

Una I'm so thrilled we're sharing a room – someone to give a hand with all those little female procedures. I've got the most marvellous device I adapted from shampoo spray . . .

Barbara Victoria! I'll be knocking on your door tonight I expect – twenty-seven years of marital grievances – I shall enjoy sharing them with you.

Joyanne *(passing photo over)* These are the men we're having dinner with tomorrow, Victoria. He on the left, Nobby – you'll like him – he's very witty. I bet you've never seen a medallion hung round that before.

Victoria *(handing it back)* No.

Kathy *(hanging over her seat)* I hope you're an early bird!

Victoria Eh?

Kathy We want you on that diving board at 6.30, don't we, Alan?

Alan Yes we do!

Kathy And don't think you can just lock the door and go back to sleep, because we're very persistent.

Alan And we're only one balcony aw– ay . . .

Victoria Mm.

Bing Bong from P.A.

Pilot *(Voice Over)* Captain Lewis again, I'm afraid. Well, we've located the source of the trouble. *(Cheers.)* We've checked with the engineers what the warning light mentioned actually indicates. Apparently it means there's a dry roasted peanut somewhere in the fuel line. *(Interested murmurs.)* So until that's pinpointed and removed, it's back to the terminal building, I'm afraid, with our apologies. *(Groans.)*

Carol bustles past, calling back to an unseen stewardess.

Carol   What do we do, Kim, wait for the bus?

On the runway. One very small bus is followed by Victoria, Joyanne and extras on top of a luggage wagon. They are singing 'One Man Went to Mow'. Joyanne is showing Victoria photos.

A café with tables outside, in bright sunshine. Victoria sits in different clothes drinking lemon tea. A Spanish waiter arrives at the table.

Waiter   Enjoy your drink, yes?
Victoria   Yes thanks.
Waiter   Beautiful weather, ehy? Nice tan for ladies.
Victoria   Yeah. How much was that?
Waiter   *(in Spanish)* One cheese sandwich, one tea with lemon. Altogether, one pound fifty *(in English)*.
Victoria   *(putting down money)* Cheers. Bye.

(She walks to her car. The café is part of a Little Chef, or another motorway services, somewhere very British and unattractive.)

Well of course I didn't go. I may be mad but I'm not stupid.

She drives away.

Over to Pam

Over to Pam

*Daytime. Victoria's car is pulling up outside a little town
house on a smart new estate. Victoria gets out, goes to the
front door and rings the bell. Lorraine shouts through an
upstairs window.*

Lorraine   I'm just drying my nails!
Victoria   OK. *(To us.)* You know daytime television? You know
what it's supposed to be for? It's to keep unemployed
people happy. It's supposed to stop them running to the
social security demanding mad luxuries like cookers and
windows. I don't see how, though, do you? I suppose
the idea is you sit there and say, 'Well I may be out
of a job but at least I'm not standing next to a library
assistant called Meredith shouting out eight words to
do with toast.' Of course quiz programmes do help the
unemployed – because they're all hosted by people who
could never be given a job anywhere else. I won't name
names, I shall just say perm and V-neck sweater. That's
six of them for a start. I don't mind the quizzes so much
as the discussion programmes. The ones where they go,
'Yes, you – the lady with the blotchy neck – do you think
they should bring back capital punishment for parking
offences?'
'Well I don't really think so because you might hang
someone for double parking then find out it was a *bone
fide* delivery, Eric.'
You see, Lorraine – this is my friend Lorraine that I'm
waiting for – she's being interviewed on television this
afternoon, and I'm taking her because she's my friend,
and because I'm *au fait*. I'm *au fait* with television – I
am. I know them all – Katie Boyle, Sooty. I worked with
Judith Chalmers before she was brown.
This programme Lorraine's doing is called 'Live with
Pam'. It's a women's programme. I don't really like

women's programmes. I always think they're going to
whip up their pinnies and say, 'Well the incision was
from here to here, Miriam.' But this 'Live with Pam' this
afternoon, it's all about success; because Lorraine is like
the classic success story – started as a Saturday girl at the
hairdressers and now you can't have your hair washed
in this county without it being one of Lorraine's girls
soaking your polo neck and saying, 'Is the water all right
for you?'

*Lorraine comes out of the front door, slams it and runs
down the path.*

Lorraine   I'm sorry I'm sorry I'm sorry I'm sorry I'm sorry . . .

Inside Victoria's car. Victoria is reversing up the street.

Victoria   What's that perfume?
Lorraine   Isn't it vile. It's called 'Take Me'! I got it at a tupperware
party. They should have called it 'Put Me Back and Shoot
Me'. God, this bra.
Victoria   What's up with it?
Lorraine   I ordered it out the back of the *Daily Mirror*. I'd feel
better wearing a potting shed and two dozen fast-growing
conifers.
Victoria   I've never seen 'Live with Pam'.
Lorraine   Me either, but the girls at work say Pam is like really,
really warm and understanding and sympathetic.
Victoria   *(to perfectly innocent pedestrian at side of road)* Oh stop
dithering about, you chronic old trout!
Lorraine   Very much like yourself.

*Inside the reception area at Console Television. The main
feature is the desk, with seating area nearby, various
doors off, a lift, and blow-up photos of the station's
personalities. A glamorous and unattractive fiftyish
receptionist – Saundra – is taking calls, parcels, and
waving at everyone who passes by. Victoria approaches
Saundra who is in full flow on the phone.*

Saundra   Well I can try the gallery, Petra, but I don't think they'll go till the bike gets here with his toupee. I know – we're all saying it – yes, she did – I said I agree with you, Dame Judi – he's actually more attractive without it. No I won't, Petra, I'm having a yoghurt thanks. Ciao. *(She turns to Victoria and says nastily)* Yes? *(She recognises her.)* Oh I didn't recognise you. What do you want – fifth floor?

Victoria   No – we –

Saundra   *(Taking a call)* 'Scuse I. A terrapin, Nigel? Not at the desk, no. Oh it is – I thought it was an indoor plant thing. All right, Nigel – ciao.

A girl comes in from outside with a dry cleaning bag.

Is this Pam's? Isn't it gorgeous? Those little pleats are dinky, aren't they? Mm, it's to die for.

She takes the dress, and the girl goes out.

OK, Marilyn, take care. Now who did you say you . . . *(She takes a call.)* Console Television, how may I help you? Ringing for you now, Tony. When are you going to do some more lovely plays for us? No they were superb. Well that was it, Tony – they were popular and yet they didn't seem to catch on with the public. Oh you're through – ciao, Tony. *(To Victoria.)* Your last series – really super – just what we need in this miserable old environment of ours. Jennifer not with you?

Victoria   I'm Victoria Wood. I've got Lorraine Spence – 'Live with Pam'.

Saundra   Well I'll try 739 but with this flu . . . *(She dials.)* I should have been off at ten to – and it's not a nice flu – it's quite intestinal. *(She calls across to Marge.)* Marge! *(Into phone)* Yes, Miss Spence is in reception for you. Marge! They'll be down in a moment.

Marge crosses over to the desk. Victoria sits down.

You're looking marvellous – you've lost weight.

Marge   Oh I haven't.

Saundra   Oh you have. You really have. Because you were quite

hippy at one point, weren't you? What's your secret – I
won't tell anybody!

Marge   My father died, and . . .

Saundra   Did he? And you lost weight? Isn't that so funny? When
my mother passed on I really picked. I really did. Talk
about Pig Avenue. Ciao, Marge – take care.

Marge leaves.

Lorraine   *(nodding at wallmounted photo)* That's Geoffrey Paige.
He's my heart-throb. I wish I was doing his programme.
Look at his hair – the root-lift on that is fantastic.

Saundra   *(to Victoria)* I say, Victoria, I've got my yoghurt here.

Victoria   Ha.

Saundra   I have! In a polythene bag just under here.

Victoria   Ha.

Saundra   Tropical fruit!

Victoria   Ha.

*A biker comes in with toupé, hands it to Saundra
and leaves.*

Saundra   Well I hope it doesn't smell of Hamlets this time, Alan.

*Caroline, a researcher, extremely trendy, in her late
twenties, enters and looks vaguely around.*

Caroline   Dr Najitwar, Saundra?

Saundra   *(less smarmily)* She's been taken to Make Up, Caroline,
and 774 know she's been taken to Make Up so why
they've sent you here for her I do not figure. I don't
know why I bother dialling. Might as well be the Pope
for all the benefit I do on this switchboard. Except I can't
speak Italian.

Caroline   Oh I know, Saundra, I'm sorry. Charlotte's got the flu
now so . . . *(She checks her list.)* Lorraine Spence?

Lorraine   Hiya.

Caroline   'Hiya'. Sorry to keep you – it's a bit chaotic today –
everyone's got this terrible flu – I really wouldn't get it
if I were you. *(She leads the way to the lift.)* It's really
awful; people have just been throwing up like nine pins.

Sue	*(on her way to the desk)* Hiya, Caroline.
Caroline	Hi, Sue.
Sue	You know I have to have a whole new sidelight – twenty-seven pounds.
Caroline	Really? How chronic. God this lift – it's really really slow – the times they've promised to mend it. I mean, they just haven't mended it – well they're a union, I suppose they don't have to. Sorry – I'm Caroline. Charlotte, you spoke to her, yeah? Well she's off so I'll be just running through it with you, OK?
Lorraine	Yeah, OK, whatever.
Caroline	God, what an amazing accent! Is it Brummie?
Victoria	No, it's Liverpool.
Caroline	Oh hi – I didn't recognise you, I love that thing you do, God, you know, the fifties er dancing – so funny, with the handbags.
Victoria	That was French and Saunders.
Caroline	Oh right. They're really funny, aren't they? We wanted them for 'Take My Pet' but I think one of them was having a baby or something. Oh lift, brilliant.

They step into the lift. Caroline presses buttons ineptly.

Caroline	God, these doors, You could be here all day trying to get them to shut; they're really gloomy news. There's some sort of a delay I think – so if there's a fire . . .
Victoria	What?
Caroline	What?
Victoria	If there's a fire, what?
Caroline	That's right.
Lorraine	Carpet up the walls.
Victoria	Laura Ashley's Broadmoor collection.

The doors begin to close.

Caroline	See, they're closing now.
Victoria	Oh yeah.

Pam, Joan Collins' age, in Carmens and casuals, strides across the lobby with an armful of papers and a tiny tape recorder.

Pam	Hold the doors! *(She steps into the lift. They all shuffle round to make room.)* Five! *(Caroline presses the button. Pam switches on tape recorder, checking a memo.)* To Michael Soper, executive producer, 'Live with Pam'; very disturbed by your memo re proposed plan to reduce my slot from two hours to twelve and a half minutes. *(Doors begin to close.)* Darn. *(To Caroline.)* Er – get my dress. It's at the desk. Straight to my dressing room, please. Padded hanger.
Caroline	Oh sure, Pam.

Caroline starts to leave and stands wedging the door open.

Pam	*(into tape)* You describe my interviewing technique as synthetic, which, by the way, is spelt with a 'y'. *(To Caroline)* Yes!
Caroline	Oh yes – sorry – *(To Lorraine and Victoria.)* Could you sort of make your way to Make Up?
Victoria	Where is it?
Caroline	First floor – sort of just outside the lift doors and it says 'Make Up' on it in writing. Is that OK? I'll catch you later.

She slithers away; the lift doors close.

Pam	You can underline this next sentence –
Lorraine	*(whispering)* If we stay in here much longer my hair'll go out of fashion.
Pam	Please – I am dictating – a most crucial memo . . . I have never in twenty-two years broadcasting . . .

A small make up room. At the far end are an over-excited old couple, Jim and Alma, being made up for 'Chuck a Sausage', and Dr Rani Najitwar. Victoria and Lorraine enter, to be met by Sue their very nice make up lady. By Sue's place is a very elaborate blonde wig on a stand.

Sue	Lorraine? 'Live with Pam'?
Lorraine	Yeah.
Sue	Just pop yourself down, Lorraine, get yourself

	comfy, I'll just get my little sheet . . . *(She wanders away.)*
Lorraine	What shall I have done?
Victoria	Nothing, you look great.
Sue	*(as she comes back in)* OK. Right, Lorraine – here's Caroline's memo – 'nice and tarty really slap it on' – that sounds fun. I'll pop this robe on. Teresa? Have you got that new palette, 'Nauseating Neons'? It's all right, they're in my fishing bag, going blind here.
Victoria	Why is she supposed to look tarty?
Sue	I think I'll just lard it over whatever you're wearing, Lorraine.
Lorraine	All right.
Victoria	Well actually . . .
Sue	Sorry – is this wrong? This is what I was told.

Neil, a busy boy assistant floor manager, rushes in.

Neil	Chuck a Sausage? Alma? Will she be long?
Sue	Teresa's on 'Chuck a Sausage', Neil. You know it was twenty-seven pounds just for that sidelight.
Neil	God, was it? Cheers. I'm doing everybody this morning. Paula's got flu. She's lying on the props room floor like a draught excluder. *(He runs over to Teresa.)*
Sue	Well my lady'll be half an hour! She's Live with Pam. Now – *(She looks around.)*
Lorraine	Do you have to look like what they say then?
Victoria	No.
Sue	Peach finesse, where are you?
Lorraine	You tell her.
Victoria	I think Lorraine wants to look like, well, more like she looks, more or less . . . *(To audience)* Golly, I'm forthright and incisive, aren't I?
Sue	I only go by what's on my sheet. I only honestly came in two minutes ago, because someone dented my wing mirror, you see, So . . . *(Caroline comes in.)* Oh Caroline – can you sort this out? I've got 'tarty really slap it on' and apparently the lady's not too happy about it.
Caroline	Oh right. Well, fine. It's just that our other two interviewees – one's very sort of country tweedy and our lady doctor, she's quite Asian – so we thought if

you could be more, sort of, well not exactly common, but a bit *tacky*, we thought that would be sort of like a contrast, and you know, quite funny.

Victoria Well she *is* here as a top businesswoman.

Caroline Oh God, absolutely. No obviously we're not trying to say 'and now here's a sort of total sleaze-bag', it's just you know, we thought, because you've got that marvellous name . . .

Lorraine What, Spence?

Caroline No, Lorraine. It's brilliant isn't it?

Sue Would you like a few Carmens in there, Lorraine?

Lorraine Maybe a few small ones.

Sue and Lorraine busy themselves at the Carmen trolley.

Caroline *(to Victoria)* I mean 'Lorraine', it's sort of like 'Wyne' and 'Trycey', it's really sort of, I don't know *(in useless London accent)* 'Lorrine', it's really, dunno . . . *(She laughs.)*

Neil hustles Jim and Alma to the door.

Neil Now, it's right at the top of the stairs – have anything you like – put your badges on and they won't charge you.

Jim You know what I haven't had in a long while?

Alma Go on.

Jim Brains.

Alma You haven't had brains since Violet Wythenshawe moved in two doors up.

Neil Only you do need to be back in your dressing room by five to.

Alma You're never that punctilious with our privet.

Neil *(suddenly remembering)* Terrapin! *(He rushes out.)*

Caroline Oh, Neil – this is Lorraine – 'Live with Pam'.

Neil *(Voice Over)* Back in a tick!

Victoria Hey, Lorraine, do you want a bun or something?

Lorraine Oh yeah, great.

Caroline *(imitating Victoria's accent)* A boon!

Victoria Yah. *(to Lorraine)* What do you want?

Lorraine I'll have coffee and a croissant, thanks.

Caroline I have to go and look at some pop sox now, OK? But

	I'll return back and we'll go through the questions, yeah?
Lorraine	OK, fine.
Victoria	Do you want anything from the canteen, Caroline?
Caroline	No I'm on a diet thanks; I'll probably have something on Wednesday.

Victoria leaves.

Lorraine	This is creased, isn't it?
Caroline	I could get it pressed really easily actually.
Lorraine	Oh great, thanks!

She rips off her jacket to reveal a respectable T-shirt underneath.

	Ta.
Caroline	God, you're really physically uninhibited, aren't you? Is that from living in a terrace?

Lorraine thinks about that one.

In the canteen. Jim and Alma are at the counter scrutinising the hot and cold dishes carefully. They are both wearing large sausage badges with their names on. Saundra is just making her way back past them with a lemon tea. Victoria joins Alma and Jim.

Saundra	*(to Victoria)* Lemon tea! Aren't I good?
Victoria	Aha.
Alma	Hutch in, Jim. Come past, we're only dithering.
Victoria	No, you're all right.
Alma	We had pasties on the minibus but we're rumbling to beat the band now.
Jim	I say – my belly thinks my –
Alma	Jim! Bring him to a television programme, he starts naming parts of the body. Show me up.
Victoria	Which programme are you doing?
Alma	'Chuck a Sausage'.
Jim	'Chuck a Sausage' with Geoffrey Paige.
Alma	With Geoffrey Paige. Ooh, and he's friendly. If he's said

	hello once – well he's said hello once. Yes that's right. Now what are you having, Dad? Think on, we haven't got long.
Jim	*(reading)* Macaroni Cheese. Do I like Macaroni cheese, Alma?
Alma	Yes.
Jim	Am I having that, then?
Alma	No! He would if I let him. He'd wolf it down most successfully if I let him. Then the next thing you know he'd be sat bolt upright in bed shouting about Goering! Have the haddock.
Jim	Haddock Mornay – that sounds appetising.
Alma	*(to server)* Two of the haddocks please, and er cauli- with one and er –

Pam whizzes in, still in rollers.

Pam	Scusi, folks – it's rather important I'm served.
Alma	Oh no – you push ahead – we don't –
Victoria	Excuse me, there's a queue, these people haven't been served yet.
Pam	Very possibly, but I am making a television programme, and I rather think that ranks a little higher in importance than the sustenance of pensioners. You – any croissants?
Victoria	They're making a television programme too. And I'm after them anyway.
Server	There's two croissants left.
Victoria	Yes – I'll have those, thank you.
Pam	Now look. I am no ordinary well-preserved early middle-aged woman with a keen brain and an overwhelming sexual magnetism. I am Pam! Yes, Pam, of 'Live with Pam', and it is essential that I leave this cafeteria replete with the requisite number of calories in under eight and a half minutes or the most innovative and enthralling women's daytime discussion programme on network television will be off the air!
Victoria	The croissants, a coffee and a tea please.
Pam	I need those croissants. I am a borderline hypoglycaemic, diagnosed pastry-dependent and if you persist in defying me I have a simple choice: either I sink immediately into a dangerously deep coma, or I am forced to commandeer

those croissants for the sake of liberty, freedom of speech and daytime television.

Victoria licks each croissant.

Victoria You look. You only want these croissants because I've got them. If you really needed pastry at least two of these *(pointing to Carmens)* would be sausage rolls so you could pick them off in an emergency. Just because you're on television is no reason to go barging to the head of the queue like a heat-seeking missile in sling backs. And if you did drop comatose to the floor and 'Live with Pam' had to be replaced by soothing music and an illustration from *The People's Friend*, half your audience wouldn't even notice and the other thirty-seven would find the new version unbearably stimulating and have to lie down.

Pam I see. Well now you have jeopardised the health of daytime television's most caring presenter, perhaps I could be permitted to reach by you for a Wagon Wheel. Could I?

In the dressing room corridor. Victoria comes in with the tray. Sue follows with make up bucket.

Sue I think I'm getting my period. Tuh! *(She leaves.)*

Neil skids round the corner.

Victoria Excuse me – do you know which dressing room Lorraine Spence is in?
Neil *(checking his clipboard)* Is she 'Chuck a Sausage'?
Victoria No, 'Live with Pam'.
Neil 'Live with Pam'. I'm just about to flip my boko with this lot – I'm doing 'Chuck a Sausage', 'Live with Pam' and 'Take my Pet'. Lorraine Spence – thirty-two. I'll walk you down. Everyone's off with flu but me – I said, ooh I'll have it when everyone else has finished with it. I've got eight contestants, three interviewees, an alcoholic weatherman and a giant terrapin to keep track of. It's like trying to do the ironing on the *Titanic*.
Victoria Do you know where they all are?

Neil	They're in the studio, they're in the canteen, he's in the gents with a vodka and tonic.
Victoria	And where's the giant terrapin?
Neil	It *was* on a car rug. It's probably in a rissole by now. *(He stops by the door.)* Thirty-two. Please keep Lorraine here till I come to take her to the studio – one false move with Pam and she'll have my underpant enhancers for a table decoration. Oh cripes, Jim and Alma!

He rushes off the way they've just come.

Inside Lorraine's dressing room. It is the usual cell; washbasin, mirror, hard tweedy bed etc. Lorraine is now nicely made up but not dressed. Victoria comes in with tray.

Lorraine	Oh great – chuck us a croissant.
Victoria	Guess which old biddy I had to fight to get it?
Lorraine	Who?

Caroline comes in with Lorraine's jacket, another top and a filofax.

Caroline	Everything OK?
Lorraine	yeah – have you got my jacket?
Caroline	*(hanging them both on the rails)* Well what I've done, basically, I've brought the jacket, but actually this – Pam thought *(holding up a skimpy, low cut lurex top)* would look better on camera –
Lorraine	I don't normally wear that kind of thing.
Caroline	Oh sure, but Pam thought it would sort of fit in with the whole ethos type thing, perhaps.

Lorraine holds it up against her chest.

Anyway – before Neil takes you into the studio, I'll just run through the interview, because it is live . . . *(She opens filofax. Lorraine pulls a face at Victoria.)*

Victoria	You don't want to wear that, Lorraine.
Caroline	I think Pam is pretty keen –

Neil comes in.

Neil   You haven't seen a stupid old man wearing a sausage, have you?

Caroline   Sorry, clueless.

Neil goes out.

Neil   *(Voice Over)* Try wardrobe, Jackie!

Caroline   *(finding her place in filofax)* So – the interview – it's pretty much as you discussed over the phone. Early days.

Lorraine   I was a Saturday girl – yeah.

Caroline   And didn't your boss use to pinch your bum or something?

Lorraine   *(slightly taken aback)* Yeah, once, but –

Caroline   That's sexual harassment, OK, which is nice for us, so any dirt there – erm – you got married at seventeen, had a baby, lived in a council flat, very depressing obviously.

Lorraine   It was quite nice actually.

Caroline   So any vandalism stories – people peeing in the lifts?

Lorraine   They didn't.

Victoria   Not without putting a pedestal mat down first.

Caroline   Well, anything scuzzy; Pam really wants to hear about it – Valium?

Lorraine   I thought I was going to talk about building my hairdressing business from nothing.

Caroline   Oh sure. And how the pressure led to solvent abuse.

Lorraine   Eh?

Caroline   Didn't you say something here about sniffing hair lacquer?

Victoria   She's a hairdresser! Of course she sniffs lacquer. That's like accusing Fatima Whitbread of sniffing javelins.

Caroline   Well any mental problems, incest, baby battering, trot it all out – that *is* Pam's bag.

Lorraine   *(bemused)* OK. Is there a loo?

Caroline   Yeah – there's quite a bizarre situation about it actually; it's on the second floor, so you have to like go up two flights of stairs – creepy!

Lorraine   See you. *(Lorraine goes out.)*

Caroline   She's amazing, isn't she? I mean if I'd had to live in a council flat I think I'd probably, you know, just give up breathing.

Victoria   Why? Lots of people live in them.

Caroline   That's right. My really good friends have one in Stepney but they're barristers; it's more of a statement.

Victoria   I was wondering if you'd ever had a tweed sofa inserted quite a long way into your mouth?

Caroline   Mm, at a party, in Brighton.

Victoria   Lorraine! Wait for me!

In another bit of corridor leading to stairs.

Victoria   Lorraine!

She passes Saundra, who is on her way downstairs carrying a small tupperware.

Saundra   None of your skits – this is a Ryvita!

Victoria   Ha.

She catches Lorraine up, they walk together.

Are you sure you want to do this thing with Pam?

Lorraine   Eh?

Victoria   Television does funny things to people. Look at Angela Rippon.

Neil rushes by.

Neil   If you find any marbles – they're mine.

Lorraine   I'm only chatting with Pam. She's supposed to be genuinely sympathetic.

Victoria   She's not. She's the woman in the lift with the tape recorder. The day she's genuinely sympathetic is the day a piranha genuinely prefers an omelette.

They stop outside the ladies loo.

Lorraine   *(torn)* Yeah, but I want to be on television. It's been my life's ambition. I mean, you know my family; none of us have ever been on telly – except my dad's brother – and that was a photo-fit; the eyebrows were rubbish.

Ladies loo. Victoria is attempting to work the roller towel.

Victoria   Look – there's millions of ways to get on television. You can hang around a shopping centre and see if Esther Rantzen offers you a tray of peculiarly shaped vegetables. You can go on *Songs of Praise* and just open and shut your mouth with a hat on; I'll get you on *Blankety Blank* – they'll have anybody – bring your own magic marker, you can host the next series. What do you say?

Dr Rani comes out of a cubicle, and rinses her hands.

Dr Rani   Quite an interesting idea but I think I'll stick with medicine.

She pulls the roller towel; it works perfectly.

A studio corridor, outside the gents. The door is flanked by two others marked 'Studio One' and 'Studio Two'. Neil is in agitated conversation with Alma. Victoria enters.

Alma   I said he should have stuck to the cauli, they're not even his dentures you see.

Neil   Have you seen your Lorraine?

Victoria   No, she's not in the dressing room – isn't she in the studio?

Neil   *(looking at watch)* I thought things couldn't get any worse today. I've got a terrapin that won't come out of its shell, a contestant with food poisoning and an inebriated weatherman who's just insulted everyone in Wiltshire, Avon and the cloudier parts of Somerset.

Victoria   Who's got food poisoning?

Alma   It's Jim. We were going great guns to the semi-final – I was answering and he was chucking the sausages – then he keels over shouting, 'Loosen my braces, Alma, it's the haddock mornay!' He's never been right since Bispham.

Neil	Look – I can't stay, Alma, I'm needed on Pam; you go in and sit with him.
Alma	You shut your palate – I've gone seventy-three years without nudging up against a urinal and I'm not coming to it now. I'll take a seat down the end. If anybody wants me I'll be on that buffet under Pearl Carr and Teddy Johnson.

Alma moves off.

Neil	Silly old tea-towel – look, your friend Lorraine is due in that studio in two minutes on a live programme – it's my job to get her there and I've looked everywhere except the boilerman's left armpit. Don't tell me you think she's done a runner?
Victoria	I think she's done a runner.
Neil	Well that's it. I've had it. 'Chuck a Sausage' they can muddle through – anyway I live with the producer – but Pam . . . if she says, 'Please welcome Lorraine Spence,' and Lorraine Spence isn't there to be please welcomed I'm out. I won't work in this business again. I shan't be able to buff up the carafes on *Newsnight*. And we've got a mortgage. And we're halfway through erecting an outdoor dining ambience – I feel like putting a wig on and going on myself, I do. *(They stare at each other blankly.)*

'Live with Pam' studio. There is a ripple of applause from the small female audience as Pam turns to 'her' camera.

Pam	A success story from Dr Rani Najitwar there. But you don't need to be an immigrant to experience all the difficulties life can throw up. One of life's battlers, ladies – please welcome Lorraine Spence.

Victoria appears in the top rejected by Lorraine and blonde wig seen earlier, and hasty lip gloss. She sits down.

Pam	Lorraine – life hasn't been easy for you, has it?
Victoria	No, it's been rubbish.
Pam	Tell me about it. What sort of childhood did you have?

Victoria	In care . . . truanting . . . shoplifting.
Pam	You were a deprived child.
Victoria	Never had hotpants, never had a gonk.
Pam	Those hurts run deep, don't they, Lorraine. Did you turn to pregnancy as a way out?
Victoria	I had seven children before I were eighteen. But I couldn't cope. I were too stupid to cope. I kept leaving them in skips. Then I got to the housing list and the council give me my own skip – it were super, Pam!
Pam	And then you got married, didn't you, Lorraine?
Victoria	Yeah, but I were just as miserable, only with less room. He drunk, he scratched hisself, he kept pork niblets in his Y-fronts. I were a battered wife, Pam – I were in Casualty so often I had my own cubicle. But I loved him. I loved him, Pam!
Pam	You were a working mother, weren't you, Lorraine? Was it a good job?
Victoria	Oh yeah. Pickwick's Biscuits. They reckoned I had a flair for bourbons but I got a cross foreman and he put me back on dodgers.
Pam	What happened with the foreman, Lorraine?
Victoria	It were just sexual harassment, Pam – it don't matter. I don't want to disclose about it.
Pam	It's distressing I know, Lorraine – but it may help to bring it out and tell the viewers.
Victoria	Oh it's just that every so often they stripped me naked and pushed me round the boardroom on an orthopaedic sun lounger.
Pam	That's appalling, Lorraine – how often did this happen?
Victoria	Every tea break.
Pam	Really, yes, yes . . . Did you turn to any means of escape? Tranquillisers?
Victoria	Valium, Mogadon – I were living in a dream world, Pam; I were in a daze. I were even watching daytime television! Then when I got hooked on booze as well as tranks that's when it got really difficult –
Pam	Why, Lorraine?
Victoria	I were sleeping so many hours a day I couldn't get any drinking done.
Pam	We've heard from Rani how education helped her out of her very poor background to the position she now holds

	in the World Health Organisation: do you think it would have helped you?
Victoria	Not really, Pam.
Pam	Don't you think it might have made you more aware of your situation as a – and I mean this so kindly, Lorraine – as a rather feeble and inadequate member of the proletariat?
Victoria	You've lost me, Pam. You're bamboozling me with long syllables.
Pam	So you don't think CSEs as they then were, or a St John's Ambulance qualification, would have shone a little light into your murky darkness?
Victoria	Not really, no, Pam. I come clean, Pam. CSEs passed me by, Pam. You come knocking to me for a CSE, Pam – I can't give you one – cupboard's bare, like.
Pam	I thought so, Lorraine.
Victoria	Cos to be frank, Pam . . .
Pam	Oh please do be . . .
Victoria	I couldn't be frigged to get any, Pam.
Pam	That's very undstandable when you're a little bit stupid.
Victoria	I couldn't be frigged to get any, Pam – because I've got ten 'O' levels, five 'A' levels, a BA, an MA, a PhD, Grade 8 cor anglais, a wig *(taking it off)* and in insatiable desire to expose hypocrisy, amateurism and plain economy-sized rudeness on land, sea or television studio. You are the most patronising old cow to hit the airwaves since Mrs Bridges caught Ruby with her corsets on back to front, and I for one will not cease from mental fight till 'Live with Pam' is off the air.

Applause from the audience.

| **Pam** | *(fanning herself)* My handbag! I need pastry! |

She faints.

In reception. Saundra is on duty; Lorraine and Victoria are standing by a pile of prizes.

| **Lorraine** | Well I was thinking about what you said about Pam and that – and I popped into the other studio to have a look |

at 'Chuck a Sausage', cos you know I'm nuts on Geoffrey Paige. Then this old bloke conked out in the semi-final and they asked for a volunteer so I rushed up; brilliant – and as well as all these I'm getting a fridge-freezer, a dining table and a weekend for two in Hamburg.

Sue approaches the desk. Neil ushers Jim and Alma out.

Neil   I think everyone else is on the minibus so –
Alma   *(looking at the prizes)* They could have been our table mats, James Mottershead. I may forget but I'll never forgive.

They leave.

Victoria Where's your terrapin?
Neil   *(shrieks)* Great balls of fluff, I left it in the blinking urinal, licking the disinfectant! They're bringing your things round now, OK? See you!

Madge enters. Sue leaves the desk.

Saundra   Sue! Sue! What happened about your sidelight?
Sue   Twenty-seven pounds!
Saundra   And they still won't bring back hanging.
Sue   *(leaving)* I know! *(To Madge.)* Have you lost weight, Madge?
Madge   No!

She runs off. Pam, a coat draped over her shoulders, is being escorted by Caroline to a nearby seat.

Caroline I'll just check with Saundra about the cab, OK?
Pam   When you've checked and only when it has arrived and you have placed me very carefully in the back seat, you may remove your possessions from the 'Live with Pam' production office. From tomorrow morning you will be third assistant animal researcher on 'Take My Pet' and that is absolutely final and I will brook no ripostes.
Caroline Right. *(She crosses to Saundra.)*
Saundra   Pam's cab's on the way, Caroline. Pam – Pam –

	that was superb today. What a finish to a series. My goodness.
Pam	There are seventy-seven more to be transmitted.
Saundra	No, Pam – not so – I took Michael's memo while you were on air – from M. Soper, Exec Producer 'Live with Pam', blah blah, shall I read it, save you popping over? 'Further to my memo of this morning, tuned into today's transmission to witness most appalling shambles (bit cheeky!). As from now 'Live with Pam' is cancelled and your contract with Console Television (it actually says "helevision") is terminated.' Shall I put it in your pigeon hole? Oh your cab's here! Ciao, Pam.

Pam and Caroline move slowly to the door.

Caroline	Is it on the account, Saundra?
Saundra	Well no, not if Pam's been fired, you see. Have to be cash. Take care, lots of it.
Victoria	*(to Lorraine, who's been packing the prizes into 'Chuck a Sausage' tote bags)* Who are you taking to Hamburg? Geoffrey Paige?
Lorraine	No; what a let down *he* was – he wears a whacking great toupé. No, I'll take you.
Victoria	All right. *(To Saundra who's eating a biscuit.)* Bye!
Saundra	It's only a small one!
Victoria	Ha.
Lorraine	What do they eat in Hamburg?
Victoria	What do you think?
Lorraine	What?
Victoria	Pizzas, silly!

They leave.

Val de Ree

Val De Ree

The Yorkshire Moors; the Dales; the Peak District; any large expanse of walking country. In the distance are two figures striding along merrily, both with backpacks, tents, dangling mugs etc; Victoria and friend Jackie. Both are singing 'The Happy Wanderer'.

Victoria Val de ree . . .

Jackie Ha ha ha ha ha . . .

Victoria Val de rah . . .

Jackie Ha ha ha ha ha . . .

Both My knapsack on my back!

Victoria This is the life, eh? The air, the landscape, the exercise – I could go on forever. How long have we been walking now?

Jackie Ten minutes!

Victoria Shall we have a sit down?

They sit down. Jackie starts fiddling in her rucksack.

Victoria This is our heritage, this landscape you know, Jackie. It's timeless. You feel any minute now Christopher Timothy could come round that corner in a baby Austin, fresh from ramming his hand up the parts of a cow other actors cannot reach. What are you doing?

Jackie Looking for the orange juice.

Victoria No, save that. Come on. *(They get up.)* What we'll do, we'll stop at a farm and get milk. *(They start walking.)*

Jackie Can you do that?

Victoria Course. Have you never read *Swallows and Amazons*? They couldn't set foot outside their tents without loveable old farmers' wives thrusting half a pint of gold top down their necks. We might even get a bun.

Jackie What sort of a bun?

Victoria	A bun! A glass of milk and a bun type bun. Haven't you read any of those books!
Jackie	Well you know I'm a slow reader. I'm still only half way through *The Secret Diary of Adrian Mole Aged 12³/4* . . .
Victoria	I wouldn't bother. He's twenty-seven now, he works in a bank in Melton Mowbray. Look – there's one. *(Points out a white-washed farmhouse.)* I bet you there's some apple-cheeked old biddy round the back there in a gingham apron doling out the speckly eggs and the cottage cheese.
Jackie	Brilliant – let's go and get some milk then, all lovely and frothy and fresh from the udder. *(She sets off.)*
Victoria	Do you have to bring udders into it?

A very done-up farmyard, all clean white paint and hanging baskets. Victoria and Jackie are in conversation in the porch with very dim, posh girl.

Girl	Milk?
Jackie	We're on a walking weekend and we passed your farm and we thought, how lovely, fresh milk straight from the udder.
Victoria	Jackie!
Girl	You thought you wanted some milk?
Victoria	Yes, but it doesn't matter, honestly.
Girl	The thing in the carton, yeah?
Jackie	It's OK, really.
Girl	What, sort of to drink, did you mean?
Jackie	Yes – we thought this was a farmhouse.
Girl	Oh, it is a farmhouse – it's called Dendale Farmhouse.
Jackie	So we thought there might be cows.
Girl	Cows!
Victoria	The things with the four legs and the big brown eyes – go moo.
Girl	Oh, got you. I saw a documentary about them – it was amazing – Christopher Timothy was in it. It's on every week . . .
Jackie	So we thought we'd just stop and get a drink of milk.
Girl	Right. I'm on it. We don't have milk, I'm sorry.
Victoria	It's OK.
Girl	I could maybe find some Perrier –
Jackie	No, honestly, it doesn't matter – really.

Jamie appears in the doorway in shorts.

Jamie   Is there a problem, sweetie?
Jackie   No, it's all right.
Girl   These people really wanted some milk, Jamie.
Jamie   *(incisively)* The stuff in the carton, yeah?
Girl   Yeah.
Jamie   *(on the case)* Do we have any?
Girl   Not really.
Jamie   Can we get some faxed?

Back in open country, Victoria and Jackie are marching along.

Victoria   This is good, isn't it?
Jackie   It's brilliant! Wonderful idea of yours, to come camping. The air! *(She breathes in.)* Mm – pure hormone.
Victoria   Ozone.
Jackie   Well, what's hormone then?
Victoria   Hormones – you know what they are.
Jackie   What are they?
Victoria   They're women's things. You don't notice you've got them till you run out of them.
Jackie   Like split peas.
Victoria   Yeah – but if you run out of split peas you don't go red and grow a moustache.
Jackie   I might if I had time.
Victoria   Have you heard of Hormone Replacement Therapy?
Jackie   No?
Victoria   Neither have I. You know what I fancy now?
Jackie   What?
Victoria   That chocolate.
Jackie   What chocolate?
Victoria   That huge great bar in your rucksack. *(Silence.)* Have you got it?
Jackie   I haven't exactly got all of it.
Victoria   Have you been eating it? How much is there left?
Jackie   Well, just the paper.

They stop walking.

Victoria	You've eaten that huge bar of very expensive chocolate that I bought – when did you eat it? I never saw you put anything in your mouth. How did you have it, as a suppository?
Jackie	I was behind a hedge.
Victoria	You said you were having a wee. I thought you were a suspiciously long time. I imagined some latent bladder problem brought on by the unaccustomed exercise – it never crossed my mind you were crouched in the grass with your shorts round your ankles frantically gobbling Fruit and Nut.
Jackie	I only meant to have one square.
Victoria	One square foot?
Jackie	I have a problem with chocolate.
Victoria	So do I now. I want some and I can't have any.

They walk on in silence.

Jackie	Do you want to sing 'The Happy Wanderer'?
Victoria	No. I want to sing How Much Is That Piggy with the Rucksack?

Pause.

Jackie	Why are you limping?
Victoria	Am I limping? Muscle fatigue brought on by sugar deficiency, I would imagine.
Jackie	Pity there's no such thing as Sugar Replacement Therapy.
Victoria	There is. It's called chocolate. If you must know, I think I'm getting a blister.
Jackie	It's a shame you didn't soak your feet in a bowl of surgical spirit as I think I suggested earlier.
Victoria	Have you tried buying enough surgical spirit to fill a bowl? The woman in Boots thought I was a wino having a cocktail party. I had to buy a toilet-roll holder just to prove I wasn't homeless.
Jackie	Well, I'm having another wee if you'll excuse me.
Victoria	*(grabbing the rucksack)* A-ah. I'll mind this. Don't want you licking the dehydrated pasta whirls.
Jackie	I need something out of it.

Victoria	Use a dock leaf.
Jackie	I want to blow my nose.
Victoria	Use two – one for each nostril.

Further on, it is a little bleaker and windier. They are poring over the map which is in a plastic pocket on Jackie's chest.

Victoria	Well I think we're here.
Jackie	But where are the three little trees?
Victoria	No, they're not real trees – they're symbolic.
Jackie	Like Pinter?
Victoria	Look – we came up a little track like that, didn't we, and the river was there, and the little hilly thing – so we're here.
Jackie	But which way are we facing?
Victoria	Well, we want to go north.
Jackie	Which way's north?
Victoria	Towards the top of the map.
Jackie	But we've had it the other way round, to read it.
Victoria	North's always in the same place.
Jackie	Is it? Even in summer?
Victoria	Yeah.
Jackie	Right. And they didn't change it for the farmers or anything?
Victoria	No.
Jackie	*(efficiently)* OK. So north's to the top of the paper. Which way do we actually want to set off?
Victoria	This way.
Jackie	This way's north, is it?
Victoria	*(not so sure)* Yeah . . .
Jackie	How do you know?
Victoria	Well the sun goes from east to west, right?
Jackie	OK. I didn't know that.
Victoria	Well of course it does – how do you think you get sunsets?
Jackie	I thought that was the sea tipping up.
Victoria	It starts in the east –
Jackie	What, like Ceylon?
Victoria	Yeah. Then it crosses over –
Jackie	*(intelligently)* Yes, that's right – that's the equinox.
Victoria	No, this is every day.

Jackie	Right.
Victoria	So all we have to do is look at the sun.
Jackie	Yes.
Victoria	Look at the time.
Jackie	Yes.
Victoria	Then you work out where north is.
Jackie	I see.
Victoria	So what's the time?
Jackie	*(agreeing)* Yes.
Victoria	What *is* the time?
Jackie	The time now?
Victoria	No. The time Jesus first made a fitted wardrobe. What time is it?
Jackie	I don't know.
Victoria	I told you my watch was broken. I phoned you up. I said have you got a watch, you said yes I have. Didn't you?
Jackie	Yes.
Victoria	Where is it?
Jackie	In my cardigan pocket.
Victoria	Where's your cardigan?
Jackie	In my car.
Victoria	Well, if we can't find this campsite, Jackie, and I die of exposure trying to fetch help, you will have to write to Mrs Margaret Thatcher explaining how it was the country came to lose a much loved and irreplaceable entertainer. I hope you understand that.
Jackie	Yes I do.
Victoria	Right. Come on. I think this is north.

They set off.

Jackie	I'm sure you're right. In fact it feels a little bit colder already, don't you think so?

Moorland; nothing is to be seen for miles except a track, a stream, maybe a few sheep. Victoria and Jackie are unpacking the tent.

Victoria	Course, we probably wouldn't have liked the campsite if we had found it.

Jackie	Oh no, this is much more of an adventure. Just like your book, what was it – *Seagulls and Cannibals*?
Victoria	*Swallows and Amazons.* Swallows and Amazons for ever!
Jackie	What's it about?
Victoria	Well, they all go off in a boat, right – Susan and John and Roger and Titty.
Jackie	Roger and who?
Victoria	Roger and Titty.
Jackie	And this is a children's book?
Victoria	Yes. Shut up. Now – is that all the bits?
Jackie	Yep.
Victoria	You put the tent up – I'll get the water. Where's that folding buckety thing?
Jackie	I don't know how it goes up.
Victoria	No, but they're all basically the same, aren't they? You've been camping enough times.
Jackie	I've never been camping. That's why this is such a thrill.
Victoria	What do you mean you've never been camping?
Jackie	Haven't ever been; sorry.
Victoria	Jacqueline Thomson – when I met your mother did she or did she not say that as an adolescent you were always in tents?
Jackie	Intense! I was always intense! I haven't a clue about camping.
Victoria	Well your mother wants elocution lessons. I'm going to phone her up.
Jackie	She's not on the phone.
Victoria	Then I shall send her an offensive bouquet.
Jackie	Well I thought *you* knew all about it; you know all the words to 'The Happy Wanderer'.
Victoria	I know all the words to 'Climb Every Mountain' but I'm not a Mother Superior.
Jackie	Well, it can't be that difficult to put up. I'll read out the instructions and you join the bits together. Right. Take Tube A and apply to Bracket D, with flange channel outermost.
Victoria	Tube A . . . Tube A . . .

The same, later. Bits are scattered in odd groupings; Victoria and Jackie look slightly harassed.

Jackie	Right. Start again. Take Tube A and apply to Bracket D with flange channel outermost.
Victoria	Outermost. I've done that.
Jackie	*(mumbling)* Figure three . . . repeat with tubes B, F and J.
Victoria	Yes
Jackie	Figure four – then *quasi* tighten Socket Cap E until semi-protruding Locking Hinge K is engaged.
Victoria	Yes, I've done all that.
Jackie	Yes, but I think this is where we went wrong before. Is your Socket Cap *quasi* tightened?
Victoria	Yes!
Jackie	And is your semi-protruding Locking Hinge engaged?
Victoria	I think so.
Jackie	*(earnestly)* Well, check that it is engaged, Vic, because –
Victoria	What do you want me to do, ask to see its engagement ring? It clicked, didn't it?
Jackie	OK. Gather up Canvas Panel M, taking care that stitched gully faces Braided Thongings C, H and W, otherwise Waxed Proofing Flap O will be rendered inoperable. OK?
Victoria	What do you mean 'OK?'?
Jackie	Gather up Canvas Panel M –
Victoria	Which is it?
Jackie	Which what?
Victoria	Which is Canvas Panel M?
Jackie	The one with the stitched gully, obviously.
Victoria	They've all got a stitched gully, you pinhead. That's what you stick the rods up. How do you think the sides stay together – hormones?
Jackie	Gather up Canvas Panel M.
Victoria	I don't know which one it is. Stupid thing! I don't think these are bits of tent anyway. I think there's been some hideous mix-up at the factory, and these are actually the individual sections of some compulsive eater's pinafore dress. There's probably some poor woman in a back bedroom in Henley-in-Arden sobbing, and trying to squeeze her buttocks into a waxed proofing flap. It doesn't make sense.
Jackie	Oh come on. This is ridiculous. We're both intelligent people – a little bit of serious thought and we should have the problem solved in no time.

Victoria	That's what Neville Chamberlain said to Hitler.
Jackie	I keep telling you – I haven't read *Swallows and Amazons. (She pauses.)* Right, take Tube A and apply to Bracket D . . .

The same, later. Bits are scattered everywhere. They're on their knees, facing each other. Jackie is trying not to shout.

Jackie	*(very slowly)* Take Tube A and apply to Bracket D.
Victoria	Reading it slower does not make it any easier to do.
Jackie	I'm sorry – you read it out then.
Victoria	It doesn't matter who reads it out. You could re-write it as a duet for Cyndi Lauper and Placido Domingo, we wouldn't be any nearer putting up the stupid thing.
Jackie	Well I can't believe you've dragged me all the way out here without a smidgeon of technical expertise.
Victoria	What about you? Keen as mustard in the car – now it turns out you've never done anything more adventurous than step on an escalator in soft-soled shoes. What did you DO in your summer holidays for heaven's sake? Why weren't you a guide? Why *didn't* you go camping?
Jackie	I was in the Youth Orchestra. On the oboe.
Victoria	Well that fits together, doesn't it? Good God, what is a tent when you think about it – it's only four big oboes and an evening dress.

She stares at the bits of tent.

Jackie	There's somebody coming! A man!
Victoria	Does he look like he knows about tents?
Jackie	He's got shorts on.
Victoria	That's good. Have they got a semi-protruding locking hinge on them?
Jackie	Hello!

Mim and Daddy move into view; she is small, sprightly and jaunty, sixty-nine. Daddy is sixty-nine. They are both dressed for a nice day's fell-walking, in shorts and with little rucksacks.

Mim	*(breathing in)* Isn't it glorious? You can practically smell those hormones!
Jackie	*(under her breath)* You see?
Mim	Are you drinking it in? The scenery? Are you? We are. Aren't we? Daddy! Aren't we? Drinking it in. The scenery.
Daddy	There's plenty of it.
Mim	He's joking. He is. Aren't you? Daddy. Joking. He is. He's dry, is Daddy. Aren't you? He's like a dry white wine. Dry.
Victoria	We're having a bit of trouble with our tent, actually.
Mim	Hear that, Daddy? Trouble. Trouble is meat and drink to Dad. Isn't it Dad? Meat and drink. Well, not meat – we've given up due to the cruelty. Daddy has the odd Cumberland sausage but he was at Dunkirk so it's understandable. Two days on a lilo in full battle dress, it's not humorous.
Daddy	What's the problem?
Mim	See – straight to the heart of the topic. This is the man who terrorised the cardboard box industry for forty years. *(She pauses.)* Go on.
Jackie	I'm sure it's all perfectly obvious – we're probably being terribly dim . . .
Victoria	No we're not.
Jackie	We just cannot seem to fit the silly thing together.
Mim	Fret not. *Finito de fretto.* Leave it to Dad. He'll be at those instructions like an SAS man through an embassy window. You set to, Dad, and I'll break out the beverages.

The same, later. A little way from the tent and Daddy, who are out of sight behind a rise, Mim, and Victoria and Jackie sit relaxed, enjoying the view, drinking tea from Mim's Thermos. Victoria and Jackie are sharing a cup.

Mim	What a lovely weekend you're going to have – what did you call it?
Victoria	Backpacking.
Mim	Backpacking. What a phrase or saying that is! I'd walk for miles but we're tied to the Honda with Daddy's groin; and really now, he's not up to humping the equipment. Nor

	am I, to be brutal. I mean, I'm whippy for my size but I couldn't shoulder a toilet tent, come what might.
Jackie	*(finishing the tea)* That was lovely – thank you.
Mim	What do they say of tea? The cup that cleans but doth not inebri-ise.
Jackie	I hope we've left enough for your husband.
Mim	His tea drinking's pretty much censored since his operation. Excess liquid puts too much pressure on his tubular grommets apparently *(She calls.)* Are you nearly done, Dad?
Dad	*(Voice Over)* I'm just adjacent to finishing.
Mim	Course he's lucky in one way with his groin – you can't see it. I mean, if it was in a sling he'd be forever fending off queries.

She packs up the Thermos.

They're marvellous, aren't they, thermice? I won this
in a competition – had to put eight lightweight trusses in
order of comfort and adaptability; we chuckled home with
that one.

Daddy appears over the rise.

Mim	All done, Dad?
Daddy	More or less.
Mim	Isn't he marvellous? *(She straps him into his backpack. Victoria and Jackie stand by gratefully.)* And he's not just red hot in the handiwork area – he sings opera.
Victoria	He doesn't!
Mim	He does. Don't you, Daddy? Sing opera. He's always running himself down re the professionals but I say where would José Carreras be with a Rawlplug? We're all trotting up different snickets, aren't we?
Victoria	That's right.
Jackie	Well, thank you very much, that really was kind of you.
Dad	Pleasure.
Jackie	No really – thank you ever so much.
Mim	Come on, Dad, off we go, heading for the wild blue Honda. Bye!

*Victoria and Jackie wave them off and rush over the rise
to inspect the tent. They stare at it. It is up, but only half
of the rods have been used so it is only about two foot high
and very droopy. The unused rods are in a neat pile on
the grass.*

Jackie	It's not too bad.
Victoria	It is too bad. It's like a starter home for guinea pigs.
Jackie	At least it's up – I mean we can manage.
Victoria	Of course we can manage. Jesus managed.
Jackie	When?
Victoria	In the wilderness. I mean he managed for forty days and forty nights, but did he have a good time? Did he send a postcard home saying, 'Wish you were here, the weather is fabulous'? No. He was miserable. If he'd had a fortnight in a stationary caravan at Cleethorpes there'd be no such thing as Lent.
Jackie	Well I think it's very nice – I'm going to get the stove out and make some supper. We don't need all that space above our heads anyway – we'll only be lying down.
Victoria	That's true. And if you sleep chest down we can drop it another foot.

*After supper. Victoria and Jackie are sitting in front of
the tent.*

Victoria	That was good, wasn't it? *(She looks at the empty packet.)* I never knew that.
Jackie	What?
Victoria	If you dehydrate pasta whirls with cheese sauce and vegetables, put it in a packet, take it out of the packet, add back the water and cook it –
Jackie	Yeah?
Victoria	You get grout.
Jackie	Do you? I thought you got that from drinking port.
Victoria	Shall we get sorted before it gets dark? Have you got the bedrolls?
Jackie	*(rooting in the rucksack)* Yep. White or granary.
Victoria	Bedrolls.
Jackie	No, I haven't got them.
Victoria	I told you to get them out of the back of the car.

Jackie	Sorry. What are they?
Victoria	They go under the sleeping bags. If you haven't got them it's very painful going to sleep.
Jackie	Why?
Victoria	Because A, the ground is very hard, and B, the person who forgot them is going to get kicked all night.
Jackie	I bet they didn't have bedrolls in Whatsits and Amazons.
Victoria	They had palliasses. *(They look at each other.)* Don't ask.

The next morning. It is raining hard, and Victoria and Jackie are sitting in the tent opening, looking out at the weather.

Jackie	Do you think it's going to stop?
Victoria	No.
Jackie	Is there enough blue to make a sailor a pair of trousers?
Victoria	There isn't enough to make him a pair of popsox. If he wants grey trousers we could manage it.
Jackie	This is really depressing.
Victoria	Oh don't moan. We'll wait ten minutes, right?
Jackie	What then?
Victoria	Then we'll moan. Oh let's pack up and get going, shall we?
Jackie	All right. Let's just finish the crossword, shall we? *(She picks up yesterday's* Mirror. *Victoria groans.)* Nine across – where Stanley found Livingstone.
Victoria	The chippy? The lost property office? Freeman Hardy and Willis by the laces?
Jackie	Don't know. I'll leave that. Eight down: Grace Darling's father kept one.
Victoria	Scrapbook.
Jackie	Doesn't fit.
Victoria	Lighthouse.
Jackie	That's right! How did you know?
Victoria	Have you never heard of Grace Darling?
Jackie	She was in *High Society* with Bing Crosby. Twelve down: location of football's 'Accies'.
Victoria	Partick Thistle.
Jackie	Why?
Victoria	Because it's always Partick Thistle in crosswords. Put it in.
Jackie	Shall I?

Victoria Yes, come on, I want to go. *(She starts to undo the tent.)*
Jackie There's too many letters.
Victoria Well write small.

Later on. Victoria and Jackie are trudging along a deserted road. They are very wet.

Victoria Jackie – even if we get to the campsite we don't know how to put the tent up.
Jackie We'll ask some boys – it'll be good fun.
Victoria Boys? I'm thirty-six. Who do you think I am? Mrs Robinson?
Jackie No.
Victoria You don't know who I'm talking about, do you?
Jackie Yes I do. Mrs Robinson.
Victoria Who is she then?
Jackie Margaret Thatcher's mother – so squash!
Victoria We've got nothing to sleep on, Jackie – I'm not spending another night like last night; I've got to sleep in a bed. We could use your cash and go to a hotel.
Jackie You said just bring enough for two days' chocolate.
Victoria I thought that would be at least 150 quid.
Jackie Well let's hitch back to the car and go home.
Victoria Home? Jackie – we're backpacking – we're on the road. Good golly, have a bit of British grit, woman. We've got to see this thing through. Look at Sherpa Tensing and Hillary.
Jackie Who are they?
Victoria A magic act.
Jackie Well if we're not going home, and we can't afford a hotel, we'll have to go to that youth hostel.
Victoria Jackie – I have been in a youth hostel. I know what they're like. You are put in a kitchen with seventeen venture scouts with behavioural difficulties and made to wash swedes. You are locked out in all weathers from ten o'clock in the morning till eight o'clock at night and only admitted if you know all the harmony to 'Row Row Row Your Boat Gently Down the Stream'; the toast is made three days in advance and if anybody finds a raisin in their muesli they get a round of applause. And no matter where you are in the

building somebody somewhere is singing 'The Happy Wanderer'.

Jackie	Well it's that or trying to put the tent up.
Victoria	*(singing)* Val de ree . . .
Jackie	Ha ha ha ha ha . . .
Victoria	Val de rah . . .
Jackie	Ha ha ha ha ha . . .
Victoria	Val de ree . . .
Jackie	Ha ha ha ha ha . . .
Victoria	Val de rah ha ha ha . . .

The approach to the youth hostel. Victoria and Jackie are limping up to the front door. It's wet.

Victoria Course, they've probably changed a lot since I stayed in one. I should think they're probably run more like hotels now.

Jackie Oh yes. Everything very simple and plain.

Victoria *(pressing the bell)* But very hospitable and welcoming.

The door is flung open by upper-class woman, Susan, dressed in hiking boots, floral summer dress, and quilted body warmer, with wild greying hair. Years of running a youth hostel have driven her slightly mad.

Susan Can't you read? Are you quite blind? We're not not not open until six o'clock. This is not a hotel – I'm getting increasingly peeved by this persistent inability to grasp the roles of the establishment. Now shoo away with you. You may not loiter by the porch or verandah; if the weather worsens you may stand behind the gazebo and in cases of epilepsy or appendicitis you may oscillate the kitchen doorbell and request the telephone number of the nearest dental surgeon. Never, never ring this bell again, and cease leaning against the architrave; your mug is scratching the paintwork.

She slams the door.

Jackie Are you going to let her speak to you like that?

Victoria Yes.

Jackie	*(catching sight of Susan through a nearby window and dashing to it)* Quick – let's try again!

Jackie taps on the window. Susan looks at her.

	Could we just come in for a moment?
Susan	*(whipping the window open)* Say again?
Jackie	If we could just come in for a minute –
Susan	Do I have to elucidate yet further? I am not the Statue of Liberty and as printed quite clearly in the handbook this establishment is closed closed closed from ten o'clock in the morning until six o'clock at night. I am driven to near-madness by this unceasing insubordination and relentless stupidity on the part of people who are quite quite quite old enough to know better and who persist in treating these premises as if they were an hotel of the deluxe class. If I have any more examples of this continual harassment I shall telephone the National Trust. Is that clear?

She bangs the window shut and moves away.

Victoria	Come on! Round the back! Head her off! Quick.

They run round the side of the house to the kitchen door at the back of the hostel. Victoria and Jackie see Susan in the huge empty kitchen. They wave.

Victoria	Hey!
Susan	*(flinging open the door)* And?
Victoria	If we could just have a word with you?
Susan	This is not the Oxford Debating Society and I am not Dame Sybil Thorndike – there will be no indoor conversation out of hours stated, and any emergency chatter must be conducted through the drying room hatchway without boots. Has that clocked or have I to drawing-pin another memo? *(She pronounces it 'meemo'.)*
Jackie	Well, can we book a bed for tonight or something?
Susan	The dormitories are at top chock capacity – as it is I have had to place two inflatable mattresses in the Ping-Pong Lounge. There may possibly be a top bunk going a-begging at the Greywalls Hostel thirteen miles across the

valley. Now please go hither and yon – we have a lecture this evening and I am up to my shoulder bag with stress and confusion.

Victoria We've come for the lecture.

Susan I crave your pardon?

Jackie Yes – we're here for the lecture.

Susan You're here to give the lecture?

Jackie Yes.

Susan You're Miss Gough and Miss Calthwaite?

Jackie Yes.

Susan *(standing back welcomingly)* Come in, my dear girls – I didn't expect you so early. *(They take off their rucksacks.)* Come along – this is marvellous – I insist you have a hot cup of tea straightaway. Yes, a hot cup of tea and a Bakewell Segment! Connie!

They go in.

Inside, Susan's private drawing room, faded chintz etc, Jackie and Victoria are relaxing with a tray of tea.

Victoria Yes, but what are we going to do when the real people turn up!

Jackie She's not going to turn us away now – we'll just say it was a mistake.

Victoria Aren't there any more chocolate biscuits?

Jackie *(surprised)* Oh no, they're all gone. Funny, mmm, anyway, she's not going to throw us out into the night even if she's cross, is she?

Victoria Course she is – she's barmy. Tuh. There's only fruit cake left now.

Jackie It's very nice fruit cake.

Victoria It's not very nice. It's the sort you have to buy on the train when they've run out of sandwiches.

The phone rings.

Jackie Where's she gone; did she say?

Victoria She's upper-class – she could be anywhere. Probably out machine-gunning pheasants.

Jackie Peasants?

Victoria	More than likely. Oh answer it, Jackie.
Jackie	*(picking the phone up)* Hello? Could you just hold on a moment? It's Elizabeth Gough! They're just about to catch their train!
Victoria	Tell her it's cancelled.
Jackie	The train?
Victoria	The lecture. Then they won't come and we won't get found out.
Jackie	Hello, Miss Gough – I'm afraid the lecture has had to be cancelled . . . yes, it's this terrible weather. The roads are practically blocked, practically . . . oh I'm sure we will, as soon as the floods die down, yes we'll be in touch – well I'm speaking from the roof, so . . . thanks very much for phoning, so sorry – bye!
Victoria	Brilliant, Jackie. We can relax, have a nice evening. Bit of ping-pong – whip-whap.
Jackie	What about the lecture?
Victoria	Well it's been cancelled, hasn't it? They're not coming.
Jackie	They're already here: we're them.
Victoria	Oh blimey. You'll have to give a lecture.
Jackie	Me?
Victoria	Yep.
Jackie	I can't do it.
Victoria	Why not?
Jackie	I'm tired – I haven't the strength.
Victoria	Tired? You've just had seventeen chocolate biscuits, you should be tossing the Telecom tower from hand to hand.
Jackie	What is it anyway? The lecture. What's it on?
Victoria	Oh cripes, Jackie. Come on – we'll go and find a poster. *(They dash out.)*

At the youth hostel's main entrance: a large space with a closed shop, reception desk etc. Victoria and Jackie are scrutinising a large noticeboard covered in info.

Victoria	Got it! Sunday lectures.
Jackie	What's tonight's?
Victoria	They're all written in a circle, it hasn't got any dates on. 'Tales of the Hebrides' – did she sound Scottish?
Jackie	No. 'Nursing for Men': it's probably not that either.
Victoria	'Travels with a Harp' – lecture and recital: can't be

	that or she would have said, 'Where's your harp?' wouldn't she?
Jackie	What does that leave? 'Survival', exclamation mark.
Victoria	'The Russ Conway Years'.
Jackie	And 'Herbs for Health and Beauty'.
Victoria	What did she sound like on the phone? Camomile tea-ish, or as if she'd just come down the Eiger on a tea-tray, or what?
Jackie	She just sounds ordinary.
Victoria	Was she humming 'Sidesaddle'?
Jackie	No. *(They stare at each other hopelessly.)*

Susan bustles in.

Susan	Ah, there you are!
Victoria	We were just admiring your noticeboard.
Susan	We're very thrilled. Plywood. Now I'm off to supervise supper, but do feel free to dally in the environs.
Victoria	Have the lectures been going well?
Susan	Very. 'Nursing for Men' and the harp recital were particularly enjoyable – but I feel tonight's will be very special. But then it is, as you know, a mini-obsession of mine. Do call for more tea if you would like any.
Jackie	Do you have herb tea?
Susan	Oh yes – are you interested in herbs?
Victoria	Erm –
Susan	I've a lecture in October on herbs.
Victoria	Ah! *(She whistles a bit of 'Sidesaddle'.)*
Susan	Is that dear old Eddie Elgar? *(She checks her watch.)* Ah – I must fly fly fly, I'm afraid I have no ear for music whatsoever – *(running off)* 7.30 in the Activity Bay! Connie!
Jackie	It must be 'Survival', exclamation mark – she just said she's practically tone deaf.
Victoria	Since when has that stopped anyone enjoying Russ Conway?

Inside the hostel TV room. There is a small stage at one end with Jackie and Victoria sitting on it. Susan is in mid-address to a small group of hearty hikers.

Susan   So if washers-up could please please please remember
              the kitchen segment must be vacated, cloths aired, by
              9.10 at the latest. And in case anyone failed to get a slip
              in their packed lunch today, cocoa privileges have been
              withdrawn indefinitely. When we can trust hostellers not
              to write offensive remarks in the skin, they may possibly
              be reinstated. *(Cheering up)* Now – it is a very great thrill
              for me to introduce tonight's lecturers: Miss Gough and
              Miss Calthwaite are no strangers to youth hostelling,
              but they really hit the outward-bound headlines when
              they undertook to live for sixteen weeks on the remote
              island of Och na Peig in the Outer Hebrides off Miss
              Calthwaite's native Scotland.

Victoria *(mouthing to Jackie)* That's you.

Susan   Armed only with the bare minimum of provisions, Miss
              Gough and Miss Calthwaite's story of that testing time is
              at once plucky *(they pull appropriate faces)* heartwarming,
              amusing and yet very, very serious. Miss Gough and Miss
              Calthwaite!

              *Leading the applause, she steps down and sits eagerly
              nearby. Victoria stands.*

Victoria Thank you. Well, I don't know about Morag here, but
              I think my worst moment came three weeks into the
              experiment: we hadn't eaten for six days, we were cold,
              damp and morale was decidedly low. Then I happened
              upon quite a sizeable red squirrel native to Och na Peig.
              Killing it was no problem – I used the hypnosis and rubber
              band garotte technique – Morag'll be explaining that in
              full a little bit later – but the most almighty row blew up.
              I wanted to grill it with pine cones and Morag insisted on
              slipping it into her kagool to keep the chill off her kidneys.
              But perhaps we should start at the beginning. Morag!

              Victoria sits. Jackie stands.

Jackie   *(in a Scottish accent)* It was a cold wet February morning
              when Elizabeth Gough and I stepped out of the dinghy
              and looked at the bare rock that was to be our home for
              the next 112 days . . .

Later on, hikers are milling about eagerly discussing the lecture. Victoria and Jackie are talking to Susan.

Susan   So inspiring! Really. When you fended off the rabid seal with the rubber glove.

Victoria   It had to be done.

Susan   And I certainly never realised bladderwrack could be so appetising, Morag . . .

Jackie   Och yes!

Susan claps her hands.

Susan   Lights out in half an hour, people!

Victoria   Yes, we'll be glad to get to bed, won't we?

Jackie   Actually, Elizabeth and I almost prefer the bare rock to a mattress these days!

Susan   Yes, I thought that: I'd already decided not to insult you by offering you bed and board here.

Victoria   No it's all right –

Susan   I wouldn't be so insensitive. But do please please pitch your tent anywhere in the grounds. I can't promise you your particular favourite seagull, but we have limitless nettles and I daresay you'll happen upon the odd nutritious little vole! Now where is your tackle? Connie?

That night on the hostel lawn. The tent is in bits as before. Victoria and Jackie are staring at it.

Victoria   Right, Jackie. Take Tube A and apply to Bracket D with flange channel outermost . . .

Staying in

Staying in

Inside Victoria's living room. It is night and the room is lit by television set only, so only thing to be seen is a sofa with Victoria on it, watching TV. A brief shot of a TV picture shows a blonde woman opening a door; then back to Victoria.

TV soundtrack
male voice   I came to return your coffee
Female voice So I see. Do you always carry jars of coffee stark naked?
Male voice   When it's Café Blend, who needs underpants?

The phone rings. Victoria presses the remote control to cut off TV sound and answers it.

Victoria   Hello? Hello, Jane! *(To us)* Bossy friend! I'm watching television. It's a film with James Robertson Justice, Joan Sims, Hattie Jacques and Norman Wisdom. Who directed it? Ingmar Bergman *(To us)* She's an intellectual – it's a shame.
    What sort of party? A cocktail party. Of course I don't want to go to a cocktail party; it's number two on my list of things I never want to do. Eh? Sharing a jacuzzi with Mrs Thatcher, and number one is plumbing it in . . . I don't want to go, Jane. Because if I wanted to stand around with a load of people I don't know eating bits of cold toast I can get caught shoplifting and go to Holloway . . . I know I never go out – that's because I have a nice time staying in. There isn't a cocktail party in the world that can compete with a baked potato and the *Antiques Roadshow* . . . Well you may not find it stimulating, but the expression on the face of some avaricious old bat who's just been told her Rubens is

from the British Home Stores gets my pulse up till at least Tuesday. Yes, yes, yes. *(To audience)* Now she's saying it's about time I mixed with people of a higher mental calibre like the ones at this party.

Yes I know. I know I've got a degree. Why does that mean I have to spend my time with intellectuals? I've got a life-saving certificate but I don't spend my evenings diving for a rubber brick with my pyjamas on . . . I haven't got anything to wear . . . It's got baked potato down it . . . Well I haven't . . . I don't know when I last went to one, but I remember when people danced, the breeze from their loon pants kept blowing the joss sticks out . . . A party dress? I haven't worn a party dress since they gave you a bit of cake to take home in a serviette. Anyway, I'm not going, Jane, thank you . . . Will you take no for an answer . . .? Well, will you take *(raspberry)* for an answer . . .? It's the same answer but not so easy to spell. *(To audience)* Now she's saying she's got nobody else to go with . . .

You've got millions of friends. They can't all be ski-ing, the Alps would tip over. All right, well it better be good. I've got to go. Norman Wisdom's standing on the edge of a swimming pool and I can't imagine what's going to happen next. Bye. *(She puts the phone down.)* Bum! *(She turns TV sound back up.)*

TV soundtrack Aaaargh! *(Splosh!)*

A street of grand detached houses at night. Inside Jane's car, Jane is doing last minute make-up adjustments. Victoria is sitting in the front passenger seat. Jane is elegant and bespectacled and rather brisk.

Jane   I honestly don't see why you're so apprehensive. It's only a party.

Victoria   I don't know anybody. I'm shy. I know you consider it a wasted week if you haven't shared cheese straws with at least twenty-three total strangers but I like to be with people I know.

Jane   Like Norman Wisdom.

Victoria	If Jimmy Edwards is busy, then yes.
Jane	Anybody would think you'd never been to a party.
Victoria	I've been to them. I've been to many a teenage party where the boys would be sick in the garden and the girls would dig it into the herbaceous border with a spaghetti spoon.
Jane	I hope that won't happen tonight.
Victoria	Well I've brought one just in case. But the best one was when I actually ended up in the spare room under the coats with an apprentice fitter called Martin.
Jane	That was good?
Victoria	Except they were maxi coats. After twenty minutes we had to be lifted clear by the fire brigade.
Jane	Well; Moira is famous for her Christmas parties.
Victoria	Moira?
Jane	Yes, Moira! Anything wrong?
Victoria	No. *(She pulls a face. Jane doesn't see.)*
Jane	This is my first invitation – I'm very honoured. She's very intelligent, cultured, musical and I would say an inspired and very creative hostess.
Victoria	So we won't be doing the hokey-cokey.
Jane	You go and ring the bell – I'm not entirely happy with my lip-line. Shan't be a moment.
Victoria	OK.

She gets out of the car and goes towards a grand Georgian house with a Christmas wreath on the front door. She rings the door bell. Moira, an extremely well preserved fifty, flings the door open welcomingly. Her face drops when it's nobody she recognises.

Moira	Carols?
Victoria	Sorry?
Moira	Well one verse only, please. *(She pauses.)* Come on, 'Once in Royal David's City', chip chop.
Victoria	*(singing)* Once in Royal David's city Stood a lowly cattle shed Where a mother laid her baby In a manger for his bed. Mary was –
Moira	Thank you so much. Do drop by another time and

give me the dénouement. *(She makes to shut the door, then stops as Jane joins Victoria.)* Jane! How lovely! *(They kiss.)*

Jane   Moira. This is the friend I told you about.

Moira   Oh is it. The comedienne! I see. *(She decides not to pursue it.)* Well, come in – let the merrymaking commence. Ha ha. *(She stands back to let them in.)* Ailsa will take your coats. She used to live in a cardboard box, you know!

The entrance hall, leading through to a large drawing room: very House and Garden. *Victoria and Jane are handing over their coats to Ailsa, the young Scottish housekeeper.*

Victoria   Thanks.

Jane   Now just go in and be yourself.

Victoria   I wasn't going to go in as Al Jolson.

Jane   No, but throw yourself into the party, really let yourself go; jokes, routines – people will love it.

A small Philippino waitress proffers a tray of drinks. They each take one.

Victoria   Thanks.

Jane   *(speaking as if the waitress were senile and deaf)* Thank you. Is this champagne?

Waitress   *(thinking)* Merry Christmas. *(She leaves.)*

Jane   Now I'm going to seek out Moira – there's a little career move I think she may be able to help me with. Why don't you start with that group over there? Go and introduce yourself.

She pushes Victoria into a group of two men and two women in the doorway. She hovers by them; they smile but continue with their conversation.

First man   Of course, the marvellous thing about investing in sheltered housing is that you're never going to run out of old people.

Second man   Renewable resource, ah ha.

First woman   I don't think people are as old these days, do you?
Second woman Do you know, I'd never thought of that.
Second man   Oh I think people are living longer, Dulcie, don't you?
Second woman Well you say that, Gerald, but you look in the *Daily Telegraph*; you'll still see an awful lot of deaths.
First woman   Even quite poor old people go to Spain for weeks and weeks in the winter now.
First man   I believe so.
Second woman Now I never knew that, Hilary.
First woman   Oh yes. Months and months for threepence a week practically.
Second woman Nice places, or . . .?
First woman   Oh no. Nowhere one would want to go oneself . . . It was on the television. I was only half attending, I was waiting for the wildlife programme.
First man   Yes, we don't view a tremendous amount, but David Attenborough I do not like to miss.
First woman   Yes, he communicates so well.
Second man   He's a first-rate communicator, no doubt about it.
First woman   Apparently he's related to Richard Attenborough.
Second woman Now, I never knew that Hilary.
First woman   Oh yes. I think they were at school together.

Moira whizzes in.

Moira   Everybody hunkydory?
First man   Super show, Moira.
Second woman Lovely party.
First woman   Gorgeous tree. Did you dress it?
Moira   No, I simply ordered fistfuls of tartan ribbon and set the Philippinos on to it.
Second woman It's very effective.
First woman   Yes, because it's Christmas and yet Scottish.
Moira   Well that was a little gesture for Ailsa, she's from 'overr therr borrderr' as they say up there. She used to live in a cardboard box you know.
Second woman How marvellous.
Moira   Have you all met? Gerald, Hilary, Dulcie, Charles, this is Victoria. She's a comedienne! Yes! On telly. Now you must excuse me. I must just check . . . there's the most marvellous man – I shall bring

him over in two ticks – his name's Jim and he's a miner! Yes!

Second woman I don't know where you find them, Moira.

Moira I know! I surprise myself sometimes! Excuse me.

She bustles off. There is a slight pause.

First woman So you're a comedian?

Victoria Yes.

First woman *(as she turns)* I don't think I've ever met a comedian, have I, Gerald?

Second man Who was that chap in Barbados, then?

First woman He was a plasterer.

Second man So he was.

Second woman How extraordinary!

First man On television, eh?

Victoria Yes.

First man One thing I've always wanted to know . . .

Victoria Yes?

First man I've never met anybody who could tell me this . . .

Victoria Yes.

First man What happens to the prizes they *don't* win? What do they do – send them back?

Second man And are those David Attenborough's own safari jackets?

A deserted part of the entrance hall. Victoria is skulking about. Alan, a huge, bull-necked, aggressive Yorkshireman, detaches himself from the crowd and joins her.

Alan Sickening, bloody sickening.

Victoria I beg your pardon?

Alan Southern parasites. Licking the fat of the land while the north lies dying. Close the conservatory door, lad, there's bones inside.

Victoria Nice tree.

Alan Are you from the north?

Victoria Yes.

Alan I can tell. There's a pain behind the eyes, a sob in the

	voice. I never marched from Jarrow but those men's feet ache in my heart.
Victoria	What are you getting for Christmas?
Alan	What's any Northerner getting? Misery, hopelessness, an empty selection box and a rotten orange.
Victoria	I'm getting stabilisers for my bike!
Alan	*(coming out of his reverie)* Alan Hammond! Yorkshireman, writer, surgeon. My pen's my scalpel. I'm excising the cancer of complacency and I don't give a toss about post-operative complications.
Victoria	You write plays, don't you?
Alan	I write the truth. I write the misery, the hopelessness, the empty selection box.
Victoria	Mm.
Alan	OK – I write plays. But do you know what I write them for?
Victoria	The money?
Alan	The people. The dockers, the railwaymen – the north. I love it. I love it! I feel passionately about it. They're choking it to death and I'm saying, 'Rage, rage against the dying of the light,' because they're killing it. They're letting it die – my north.
Victoria	Whereabouts do you live?
Alan	Chiswick.

Moira swoops down on them.

Moira	Now this is very mischievous of you, skulking away out here like a sculpture – now follow me. *(She leads them away.)* Everyone's dying to meet you both. I've been telling everyone about your new play, Alan – what was it called again?
Alan	*Buttocks.*
Moira	So t'was. *(She stops and drops Victoria off at a chaise longue with Judith and Julia on it.)* Now this is Victoria – she's a comedienne! On telly! Yes! Julia and Judith, by the way. Now have you had Jim, the miner?
Julia	Yes – he was sweet.
Moira	Yes, isn't he? And surprisingly clean, I thought. Now I have a rock star somewhere for you to meet later

and I shall bring Alan back in a moment. He wrote that marvellous play with the slag heap.

Judith That does sound fun.

Moira Come along, Alan. *(She has a sudden thought.)* You've had Jim the miner?

Julia We've had the miner, but not the rock star.

Moira I shall bring him forthwith. Pip pip.

Judith and Julia make a space between them for Victoria. She sits.

Judith So you're in showbusiness? Gosh!

Victoria Yes.

Julia I should think it's jolly hard work, isn't it?

Victoria Yes.

Judith But fun?

Victoria Yes.

Julia Yes, jolly hard work but lots of fun.

Victoria Yes.

Julia Marvellous. *(Pause.)* Did you ever meet Dickie Henderson?

Victoria No.

Julia He always seemed very nice, I thought.

Victoria Yes.

Judith Was he the one with the handbag?

Julia No, that was Eric Morecambe.

Judith Eric Morecambe?

Julia Of 'The Two Ronnies'.

Judith Ah yes.

Julia Did I hear Moira say you were a comedienne?

Victoria Yes.

Judith But you don't actually tell jokes?

Victoria Yes.

Judith Good heavens!

A pause.

Julia Now I saw something that was supposed to be funny – what was it? – there was a very tall man, and a little foreign waiter in some sort of hotel.

Victoria 'Fawlty Towers.'

Julia	That's right. My cousin said, you must watch it, it's set in Torquay; but I saw about twenty minutes and quite frankly it could have been set anywhere. What a shambles!

A pause.

	We really only have television for the news and the wildlife programmes.
Judith	And the nanny!
Julia	*(in her idea of a northern accent)* Nanny couldn't do without t'telly!
Judith	I do think David Attenborough's the most marvellous communicator.
Julia	Yes, he radiates enthusiasm.

Victoria leaves the sofa; they don't notice.

Judith	And I would imagine he's a tremendously nice man.

A staircase rising from the hall. Victoria is sitting alone by some potted palms. Jane runs up.

Jane	There you are!
Victoria	Hello.
Jane	You're supposed to be mingling.
Victoria	I've mingled.
Jane	Well mingle some more.
Victoria	I'm no good at it.
Jane	What would you do if everybody came out and sat on the stairs?
Victoria	I'd hutch up.
Jane	I bring you to this beautiful house, the cream of café society; I do think the least you could do is make an effort to sparkle and not lurk in the greenery like a wallaby. Now I must find Moira; her husband could be rather useful to me. But I shall be checking up on you, so get back in there and effervesce!
Victoria	Mer mer mer.
Jane	What did you say?
Victoria	Nothing.

She plods downstairs under Jane's watchful eye to rejoin the party.

A busy part of the drawing room. A group comprising Dulcie, Hilary, Charles, Gerald and others is in full cry. It is some drinks later. Victoria hoves in, madly smiling.

Victoria *(in a voice similar to theirs)* Hello! Marvellous party!
Dulcie Yes, isn't it?
Victoria I was admiring the tree earlier.
Hilary Apparently one of Moira's little Philippinos did it.
Victoria How marvellous!
Dulcic I was just saying, I wish we could run to a Philippino. Moira says they work all the hours God sends and all on little bits of leftovers!
Victoria Good heavens.
Hilary I'm sure we met earlier but I haven't a clue what you do – isn't that awful?
Charles Hilary's supped bloody well and not very wisely!
Hilary Rotter.
Dulcie We were just discussing kitchens. Are you into kitchens?
Victoria Yes, I've just had a new one put in.
Dulcie Oh, who did it? Crummets of Winchester?
Victoria No, I met the man from Crummets of Winchester but I thought he had flimsy knobs so I plumped for Withy's of Totnes.

A general chorus of 'Withy's of Totnes, they're the best, how marvellous' etc.

Gerald Withy's are not cheap.
Victoria No, they're not cheap but they do do the whole thing for you and really I think sixty-five thousand pounds is worth it because you never have to meet the labourers.
Charles What is it, pine?
Victoria We pondered over distressed teak, but we wanted a

	farmhousey feel so we edged back to pine. And where we live is very rural so . . .
Hilary	Oh, where's that?
Victoria	It's a little village just off the Kingston by-pass.
Dulcie	Oh lovely! And Withy's of Totnes use genuine old pine don't they?
Victoria	Oh yes. All from old buildings. You flick through the brochure, see a church or chapel you particularly like, and they demolish it for you.
Gerald	Yes, that's very good, isn't it?

Moira comes in with Kevin, a young, Phil Collins type rock star.

Moira	Now this is Kevin. He's a rock star! Yes! Three number one records in America.
Kevin	*(shyly)* Hello.
Charles	We've had Kevin, actually.
Moira	Oh, you've had Kevin. In that case I shall take Kevin away pronto? Have you had Jim the miner.
Dulcie	Oh no, we haven't had a miner.
Moira	Well, I shall deliver Kevin elsewhere and bring you Jim the miner. He paints welders! Everyone all right for *hors d'oeuvres*?

There are cries of 'delicious'.

Moira	My housekeeper made them. Ailsa. She used to live in a cardboard box, you know. Right – come on, Kevin, I'll swop you with Jim . . . and I did have a comedienne somewhere . . .
Dulcie	That sounds fun.
Moira	Yes, doesn't it. She'll be telling jokes later and Kevin will be singing! *(She drags him away.)*
Kevin	Well that's a bit difficult actually . . .
Charles	Well, call me old-fashioned but I don't like to see a woman telling jokes.
Hilary	Charles thinks women aren't funny.
Gerald	Well, I'm sorry; I agree.
Hilary	But there are hundreds of funny women. There's the

	woman who does the column in the *Sunday Telegraph* for a kick-off.
Charles	Well you name me a funny woman who's attractive with it.
Dulcie	Attractive narrows it down.
Charles	You see.
Hilary	Got it!
Charles	A funny woman you wouldn't kick out of bed?
Hilary	Felicity Kendal!
Dulcie	Oh, Felicity Kendal.
Hilary	She's so sweet, isn't she?
Gerald	She makes *me* laugh.
Dulcie	So funny in that thing with the man from the other thing.
Hilary	And I always imagine that she's a tremendously nice person.
Victoria	Oh yes.
Dulcie	Do you know her?
Victoria	Yes I do – and do you know, she makes all David Attenborough's safari jackets.

Moira comes back in with Jim, a fiftyish small, sweet little man.

Hilary	How lovely.
Moira	Are you the people who hadn't had Jim?
Gerald	Yes – we'd had Kevin –
Moira	The rock star – but you hadn't had Jim. And have you had Alan?
Charles	Alan?
Moira	The playwright. He's having the most tremendous success with his clever *Buttocks*.
Charles	No, he hasn't reached us yet.
Moira	Well, he's edging through the throng your way, and he's very kindly offered to give us all an extract from his *Buttocks* a little later on. So this is Jim – he's a miner and he also paints pictures of welders – isn't that cunning? Do excuse me.

Moira goes out. Jim stands sheepishly.

Hilary	So how's life down t'pit?
Jim	My old pit's closed down actually. I pretty much paint for a living now.
Dulcie	I suppose a lot of pits have closed down, have they?
Jim	A fair few.
Dulcie	I suppose there's not the demand for coal that there was.
Jim	No, maybe not.
Dulcie	I suppose what has happened is we don't really need coal now we've got electricity.
Jim	Mm.
Jane	*(coming in)* Hilary!
Hilary	Jane! *(They kiss.)* What do you think of the party?
Jane	I'm having a splendid time. Are you?
Hilary	We were thinking of moving on, actually. Eleanor Spencer's starts at nine and she supposedly has Morris dancers and at least one Dimbleby.
Jane	Oh but you must stay for our alternative comedienne – *(She looks at Victoria.)*
Victoria	Oh, who is that, Jane? I hope she's not one of those terrible feminists holding the government up to ridicule.
Jane	Could I have a word with you?
Victoria	Yes, do excuse me. *(Being dragged away)* So thrilled to meet you, Jim – you must show me your Davey lamp . . .

In the plush cloakroom, Jane faces Victoria angrily.

Jane	What on earth were you doing?
Victoria	I was mingling and effervescing. I was doing jolly well, I thought.
Jane	And did you tell them you were a comedienne?
Victoria	No. It doesn't work. Either the conversation grinds to a halt or they tell you some long story about a dog being run over and say, 'Now that would make a jolly good sketch!' So I decided to just fit in with everybody else.
Jane	You're not supposed to be fitting in.
Victoria	Why not? I got in enough trouble for clutching the banisters.

Jane	Because you are supposed to be a novelty.
Victoria	What do you mean?
Jane	I needed an invitation to this party because I'm trying to deal with Moira's husband; I was invited on the understanding that I brought with me a raunchy, anarchic, foul-mouthed, alternative comedienne.
Victoria	Why?
Jane	Because the one Moira had found had dropped out to play Dick Whittington in Windsor.
Victoria	Right.
Jane	Which is why I thought of you.
Victoria	Right.
Jane	And if you don't get out there and launch into the old men's willies and Thatcher routine you're going to put me in an impossible position.
Victoria	Right.
Jane	If I let Moira down, I haven't a hope of pulling off this deal with her husband.
Victoria	They're getting divorced.
Jane	How do you know?
Victoria	One of the Philippinos told me.
Jane	You don't talk to Philippinos – you hand them your used cutlery. Oh. So Moira's not a blind bit of use to me anyway.
Victoria	Isn't she?
Jane	*(looking at her watch)* Well I may as well slip straight round to Eleanor Spencer's. I shan't be driving you home, all right? Bye. *(She leaves.)*
Victoria	*(thinking)* Bye. She wasn't very nice was she, boys and girls?

In the drawing room Alan is holding forth to a bemused group; Judith, Julia and others. The party is thinning out. In a corner is Kevin showing Victoria and Jim photos of his baby. In the background Moira is calling despairingly to leaving guests.

Moira	Must you go? It's barely nine. We're having a play-reading and rock singing and raunchy comedy . . . Oh well, Merry Christmas anyway.
Alan	Writing's not an art with me. It's a job. A craft. I graft

at it. They call me a writer, but I'm really a grafter; I'm a lathe operative, turning words. I'm a panel beater, hammering sentences into shape . . . I'm a master baker –

Julia   That's fascinating. And have you ever worked with Felicity Kendal?

Moira   *(directing Philippinos)* Yes, chairs round the piano, Doris, please. Chip chop, Phoebe. Everybody! *(She claps.)* Now you all know Alan Hammond's *Buttocks*. Yes? Well, he's very kindly offered to perform one half for you this evening, so gather round; then we'll have some very alternative comedy, followed by lovely, lovely rock singing and then Jim our little miner will be doing instant portraits in the orangery. So get a drink and settle down.

A general kerfuffle.

Victoria   Did you offer to do portraits, Jim?

Jim   Did I heck! Anyway, I can't do noses. That's why I paint welders.

Kevin   He's twelve weeks old here. You can see he's completely different to what he was at eleven weeks.

Victoria   Ah, he's sweet.

Moira   Lights down, Doris please. *(The lights dim. Alan takes up a position in front of the seated guests.)* Mr Alan Hammond and his *Buttocks*.

Moira stands to one side attentively.

Alan   The stage is in darkness. The silence is broken by the noise of an eighteen-stone riveter retching into a rusty bucket. *(Murmurs of distaste.)* Lights up to reveal Spud, a mentally defective window cleaner, naked except for a bobble hat and fingerless gloves. He speaks. (I want my mam! Mam! Why did they put you in that box, Mam? Why were you so cold, Mam? Mam! I don't like it on my own. They're giving me funny looks, Mam. And I can't find my underpants . . .)

Jim   I can't stand much more of this.

Victoria	Nor me.
Kevin	It's you next.
Victoria	I'm not doing it, are you?
Kevin	Well – I don't know how to say no.
Victoria	Let's hide.
Kevin	Where?
Victoria	I know. Follow me.

They creep out behind floorlength curtains. Rustles and uncomfortable coughs from audience.

Alan	Enter Lana, a one-legged prostitute from Tiger Bay. *(In Cardiff accent)* All right, lovey?

In the kitchen. Kevin, Jim, Victoria and Ailsa are sitting round the table with a pot of tea, playing cards. A very jolly atmosphere. Radio Two is playing organ music.

Kevin	*(obviously for the seventeenth time)* Er – what's trumps?
Other three	Spades!
Kevin	Bother!

He puts a card down, the others follow suit, and Ailsa takes the trick.

Ailsa	Thank you.
Jim	You've played this before, Ailsa.
Ailsa	When we were sleeping rough there wasn't a lot else to do.
Victoria	What was it like, living in a cardboard box?
Ailsa	It wasn't too bad. At least mine had all its flaps. More tea anybody?
Victoria	Please.
Jim	Is there any more shepherd's pie?
Ailsa	Help yourself. Doris made it. She's from the Philippines but she's really got to grips with mince.
Kevin	*(pushing the photos over)* That's my baby, Ailsa.
Ailsa	Oh yeah – I read you'd had a baby. What's the stuff in the bowl?

Kevin	That's the placenta.
Ailsa	It's nice.
Kevin	Yeah, I never thought much of placentas before but I really like that one.

Moira enters rather agitated.

Moira	Oh there you are! I couldn't begin to think where you'd gone. I think Alan is approaching an interval, or what one might describe as a cleft in his *Buttocks* and I rather fear if we don't nip in quick and plug the gap he will carry on with the entire second half. *(She waits, then gestures.)* Coming along, yes? *(Jim and Kevin look down at the floor, Ailsa busies herself at the sink and turns the radio off.)*
Victoria	No.
Moira	I beg your pardon?
Victoria	We don't want to.
Moira	I'm not with you.
Victoria	Jim doesn't want to do any portraits, Kevin doesn't want to sing and I don't want to tell any jokes.
Moira	Well I'm sorry – we all have to do things we don't want to do. I don't particularly want to be the most successful hostess in London society but that is the furrow I have been given to plough, and plough it I will.
Victoria	But we're your guests.
Moira	So I see. You're quite happy to yomp your way through a quarter of Darjeeling and sit down here while that dreadful Yorkshireman brings my entire party to a shuddering halt. *(She pauses.)* Have I read the situation aright?
Victoria	Yes.
Moira	I see. In that case there's nothing more to be said but BAARGH! *(She bursts into tears and runs out.)*
Victoria	Someone'll have to go after her.
Ailsa	Well I can't.
Kevin	I can't, I can't bear people crying.
Jim	I'd be useless. It's not even as if she was a welder.

Victoria sighs and goes out.

In the cloakroom Moira is mopping up her make-up.

Victoria	It's not anything against you – it's just that we want to relax and enjoy ourselves like everybody else. You do see.
Moira	Oh yes. *(She sniffs.)* What do I look like? Barbara Cartland without the vitamins comes pretty darn near. It's just one has been rather known for one's parties and it's harder and harder to keep going, with Eleanor Spencer coming up on the rails with her Morris dancers – and then there's this stupid divorce; not a very nice way to end a marriage. I shall be lucky to come out of the settlement with a five-bedroomed cottage in Wiltshire and one Philippino.
Victoria	Which one will you keep, Doris or Phoebe?
Moira	Oh Doris, undoubtedly. Phoebe's sex mad, which I don't mind *per se*, but it affects her ironing. So this was somewhat in the nature of a last bash, but it seems to have turned into something rather less festive than the three-day week. Any bright thoughts?

In the drawing room. Victoria is playing the piano and all the guests, including Moira, Alan and Kevin are playing musical chairs. The music stops. They scramble madly for chairs, and all sit down. The music begins again. Jim is by the piano drawing a donkey to pin the tail on. Ailsa is making up a package for 'pass the parcel'. The music stops and they scramble again.

Ailsa	There's something wrong with this game.
Victoria	What?
Ailsa	They've all got a chair. We've never taken one away.
Victoria	Oh yeah. I thought it was taking a long time.

At the front door. Moira is seeing guests out. Each one is handed a piece of cake in a serviette, and most are holding balloons. Gerald, Charles, Dulcie and Hilary are leaving. There is a general chorus of goodbyes, Merry Christmasses, lovely party, etc.

Moira	Merry Christmas! Do mind your balloon.
Alan	*(storming out)* Bourgeois pillocks.
Moira	Well I'm sorry, Alan – the music stopped and your leg was wobbling.

Kevin, Victoria and Jim leave.

	Your chauffeur is just outside, Kevin.
Kevin	Cheers. Night night.
Jim	Bye. Thanks for the shepherds pie.
Victoria	Bye.
Moira	It really was marvellous – thank you so much.
Victoria	I enjoyed it.
Moira	I'm having a little dinner party soon – just eighteen or nineteen people – I'll phone you.
Victoria	OK. Night.

Victoria's living room, as before. Victoria is watching TV on the sofa, as before.

TV soundtrack voice of George Formby	Well I've never played my ukelele in a bunker before.
Female voice	Oh George, you are marvellous. And did you notice – even Hitler joined in!
George Formby	Turned out nice again.

Music from the TV. The phone rings. Victoria thinks about answering it. She doesn't and it stops. A shot of the TV screen – blonde girl is on once more.

TV soundtrack female voice	I believe I owe you a cup of coffee.
Male voice	Café blend?
Female voice	No, it's too expensive. This is from the VG shop.

Cast List

The plays in this volume were first performed in the series *Victoria Wood* on BBCTV, in the autumn of 1989.

Mens Sana in Thingummy Doodah

Victoria	Victoria Wood
Lill	Lill Roughley
Dana	Liza Tarbuck
Connie	Meg Johnson
Enid	Anne Reid
Sallyanne	Georgia Allen
Nicola	Julie Walters
Judy	Selina Cadell
Maintenance Man	Brian Burdon
Girl on video	Ros March
Man in café	Peter Martin

Guy	Tristram Wymark
Woman in car	Ros March
Woman in lift	Valerie Minifie
Man on travelator	Peter Martin
Girl at check-in desk	Susie Blake
Spanish waiter	Joe Fraser

The Library

Victoria	Victoria Wood
Sheila	Anne Reid
Ted	Danny O'Dea
Madge	Carol Macready
John	Richard Kane
Keith	Philip Lowrie
Richard	David Henry

We'd Quite Like to Apologise

Victoria	Victoria Wood
Una	Una Stubbs
John	Philip Lowrie
Barbara	Lill Roughly
Joyanne	Julie Walters
Kathy	Jane Horrocks
Alan	Richard Hope
Carol	Celia Imrie

Over to Pam

Victoria	Victoria Wood
Lorraine	Kay Adshead
Saundra	Meg Johnson
Marge	Shirley Cain
Caroline	Julia St John
Pam	Julie Walters
Jim	Hugh Lloyd
Alma	Margery Mason
Dr Rani	Charubala Chokshi
Sue	Lill Roughley
Neil	William Osborne
Server	Alison King

Val de Ree

Victoria	Victoria Wood
Jackie	Celia Imrie
Girl on farm	Sian Thomas
Jamie	Michael Lumsden
Mim	Avril Angers
Daddy	Michael Nightingale
Susan	Joan Sims

Staying in

Victoria	Victoria Wood	**Gerald**	Roger Brierley
Woman		**Hilary**	Phyllis Calvert
on TV	Celia Imrie	**Dulcie**	Lill Roughley
Jane	Deborah Grant	**Judith**	Susie Blake
Moira	Patricia Hodge	**Julia**	Celia Imrie
Ailsa	Dawn Archibald	**Alan**	Jim Broadbent
Waitress	Susan Leong	**Kevin**	Richard Lintern
Charles	John Nettleton	**Jim**	Brian Burdon

'Mens Sana in Thingummy Doodah', 'We'd Quite Like to Apologise', 'Over to Pam' and 'Val de Ree' directed by Kevin Bishop and produced by Geoff Posner.

'The Library' and 'Staying in' directed and produced by Geoff Posner.